UNDERSTANDING:

The Universal Solvent

UNDERSTANDING:
The Universal Solvent

Quotations from the works of

L. RON HUBBARD

Published in the United States by
Bridge Publications, Inc.
4751 Fountain Avenue
Los Angeles, California 90029

ISBN 0-88404-640-0

Printed in the United States of America.

Important Note

In reading this book, be very certain you never go past a word you do not fully understand.

The only reason a person gives up a study or becomes confused or unable to learn is because he or she has gone past a word that was not understood.

The confusion or inability to grasp or learn comes AFTER a word that the person did not have defined and understood.

Have you ever had the experience of coming to the end of a page and realizing you didn't know what you had read? Well, somewhere earlier on that page you went past a word that you had no definition for or an incorrect definition for.

Here's an example. "It was found that when the crepuscule arrived the children were quieter and when it was not present, they were much livelier." You see what happens. You think you don't understand the whole idea, but the inability to understand came entirely from the one word you could not define, *crepuscule*, which means twilight or darkness.

It may not only be the new and unusual words that you will have to look up. Some commonly used words can often be misdefined and so cause confusion.

This datum about not going past an undefined word is the most important fact in the whole subject of study. Every subject you have taken up and abandoned had its words which you failed to get defined.

Therefore, in studying this book be very, very certain you never go past a word you do not fully understand. If the material becomes confusing or you can't seem to grasp it, there will be a word just earlier that you have not understood. Don't go any further, but go back to BEFORE you got into trouble, find the misunderstood word and get it defined.

Definitions

As an aid to the reader, words most likely to be misunderstood have been defined in the glossary at the back of this book. Words sometimes have several meanings. The definitions used in this glossary only give the meaning that the word has as it is used in the text. Other definitions for the word can be found in a dictionary.

*The only richness there is
is understanding.*

Editors' Foreword

This book is a collection of quotations from the works of L. Ron Hubbard, one of the most highly acclaimed authors of all time.

His over 530 published works, which have been translated into more than two dozen languages, have sold over 95 million copies and have gone to the top of bestseller lists around the world, reveal an uncommon insight into mankind and the human condition. Through vigorous research and exploration into every corner of man's experience, L. Ron Hubbard developed the Scientology philosophy—a technology for handling and improving life which has helped millions of people to lead happier, more successful lives. His extensive writings and over 6,000 recorded lectures contain a wisdom which is extraordinary in its perception and power.

Mr. Hubbard's use and mastery of the language is strikingly beautiful and often poetic. Yet the real strength of these writings lies in the fact that they reflect the fundamental truths which man has been striving to discover and understand throughout the ages.

As he stated in an article entitled "My Philosophy":

"I know no man who has any monopoly upon the wisdom of this universe. It belongs to those who can use it to help themselves and others.

"If things were a little better known and understood, we would all lead happier lives."

The passages selected for this book have been assembled from many of Mr. Hubbard's published books, articles and lectures. They have been categorized for ease of reading and a full index has been included in the back of the book.

We invite you not just to read the concepts outlined on these pages, but to use them.

—The Editors

Contents

On Understanding

*L*ife
in its highest state
is understanding.

Dianetics 55!

*L*ife in its lower states
    is at a lower level of understanding,
and where life has ceased to function
    and has arrived at what one
      might call total incapability,
        there is no understanding at all.

Dianetics 55!

The only richness there is
is understanding.

Scientology 8-8008

That mind
which understands itself
is the mind of a free man.

Dianetics 55!

*You can blame
   your whole confusion
on the fact
   you bought illusion.*

The Route to Infinity Lectures:
Appendix, "Dianetics Jingles"

Because life is understanding
it attempts to understand.

When it turns and faces
the incomprehensible
it feels balked and baffled,
feels there is a secret,
and feels that the secret
is a threat to existence.

Dianetics 55!

There are conditions
worse than being unable to see,
and that is imagining one sees.

Personal Achievement Series Lecture:
"Scientology and Effective Knowledge"

There is no solution at any time
superior to the ability
of the person asking for it
to understand.

Lecture: "Gradients and ARC"

Understanding
is the universal solvent.

It washes away everything.

Lecture: *"Gradients and ARC"*

It is a truism
that if we could understand all life
we would then tolerate all life.

Further, and more germane to ability,
if one could occupy the position
of any part of life,
one would feel a sufficient affinity
for life to be able to merge with it
or separate from it at will.

Dianetics 55!

The fewer viewpoints
which an individual will tolerate,
the greater his occlusion
and the worse his general state
of beingness is.

The Phoenix Lectures

Understanding
has very specific component parts.
These component parts are
affinity, reality and communication.

Dianetics 55!

*A*ffinity manifests itself
    as the recognition of similarity
of efforts and goals amongst organisms
    by those organisms.

Scientology 0-8: The Book of Basics

*R*eality is fundamentally agreement.
*W*hat we agree to be real
    is real.

Scientology: The Fundamentals of Thought

Try to get somebody to be reasonable
when he is very angry
and you'll find out
his reality is very bad.

The Phoenix Lectures

The avoidance of reality
is merely an avoidance
of present time.

A New Slant on Life

*When we say
somebody should be in present time
we mean he should be
in communication with his environment.*

*We mean, further,
that he should be in communication
with his environment
as it exists,
not as it existed.*

Dianetics 55!

*W*hen communication starts failing
the affinity starts dropping.

*P*eople have secrets from each other
and the affinity starts out the bottom.

The Problems of Work

*Most causes for complaint
are based not on misconduct
but on misunderstanding.*

Organization Executive Course:
"Model Hat for an Executive"

*Only personal contact
can restore understanding.*

Organization Executive Course:
"Model Hat for an Executive"

On
Communication

Communication is the consideration and action
of impelling an impulse or particle
from source-point across a distance
to receipt-point,
with the intention of bringing into being
at the receipt-point
a duplication and understanding
of that which emanated
from the source-point.

Technical Bulletin: "Axiom 28 Amended"

A man is as dead
    as he can't communicate.

He is as alive
    as he can communicate.

Dianetics 55!

An individual can become so dependent upon others or entertainments in originating communications that he himself does not.

Indeed, it is very unpopular in this society at this time to originate communications.

Dianetics 55!

So that is the basic lesson
  that anybody learns in this universe.
They learn to keep their mouth shut,
  and it's the wrong lesson.
When in doubt, talk.
When in doubt, communicate.

The Phoenix Lectures

*D*o not give or receive communication unless you yourself desire it.

The Creation of Human Ability

*F*lattery is not very useful,
is often suspect,
as it does not come from a sincere belief
and the falsity in it is detectable
to all but a fool.

Management Series: "Manners"

*C*ommunication is essentially something
which is sent and which is received.
The intention to send
and the intention to receive
must both be present in some degree
before an actual communication
can take place.
Therefore one could have conditions
which appeared to be communications
which were not.

Scientology: The Fundamentals of Thought

It could be said
 that all the entrapment there is,
  is the waiting one does for an answer.

Dianetics 55!

*S*ome people *have* to talk.
With this compulsion
   they are out of communication.

Communication is a two-way affair.

Notes on the Lectures
of L. Ron Hubbard

What is a secret?
It is the answer
which was never given,
and this is all a secret is.

Dianetics 55!

*Communication is the root
of marital success
from which a strong union can grow,
and noncommunication is the rock
on which the ship will bash out her keel.*

A New Slant on Life

*He who would outflow
must inflow—
he who would inflow
must outflow.*

Dianetics 55!

*Unless one can originate communications
one's imagination is in bad shape.
The reverse does not happen to be true.
The imagination is not that thing
which is first imperiled
and then results in failure
to originate communication.
Failure of communication origin
then results in failure of imagination,
so the rehabilitation
of communication origin
rehabilitates as well the imagination.*

Dianetics 55!

*Perhaps the most fundamental right
of any being
is the right to communicate.
Without this freedom,
other rights deteriorate.*

Introduction to Scientology Ethics

*No wise man should stammer
because another shuns his grammar.*

The Route to Infinity Lectures:
Appendix, "Dianetics Jingles"

*H*e who can truly communicate
to others
    is a higher being
        who builds new worlds.

Article: "Communication"

*F*or a very great many years
I asked this question,
"To communicate, or not to communicate?"
If one got himself in such thorough trouble
by communication,
then of course
one should stop communicating.
But this is not the case.

If one gets himself into trouble
    by communicating,
        he should further communicate.
More communication, not less,
    is the answer,
        and I consider this riddle solved
           after a quarter of a century
              of investigation and pondering.

Dianetics 55!

On
Survival

*The dynamic principle
of existence
is survival.*

Dianetics: The Modern Science
of Mental Health

*The thrust of survival
is away from death
and toward immortality.*

Dianetics: The Modern Science
of Mental Health

*M*an thrives, oddly enough,
only in the presence
of a challenging environment.

Management Series:
"Conditions, ·How to Assign"

The goals of man, then,
stem from the single goal of survival
through a conquest of the material universe.
The success of his survival
is measured in terms
of the broad survival of all.

Handbook for Preclears

*L*ife is a group effort.
*N*one survive alone.

Introduction to Scientology Ethics

A man who is known to be honest
is awarded survival—
good jobs, good friends.
And the man who has his ideals,
no matter how thoroughly
the minions of the devil
may wheedle him to desert them,
survives well only so long
as he is true to those ideals.

Self Analysis

Evil is that item or activity antipathetic to the survival of oneself and his fellows.

Personal Achievement Series Lecture:
"Man: Good or Evil"

Without order nothing can grow or expand.

Organization Executive Course:
"Administering Justice"

In life,
the only real guarantee of survival
is *abundance*.

Self Analysis

*A*s for ideals, as for honesty,
as for one's love of one's fellow man,
one cannot find good survival
for one or for many
where these things are absent.

Self Analysis

*Man, in affinity with man, survives,
and that survival is pleasure.*

Dianetics: The Modern Science
of Mental Health

Share action with a group or person
in your life,
agree to mutually survive
by some specific code
and then be cruel to them
and so transgress
and you'll have pain.

Technical Bulletin:
"Clean Hands Make a Happy Life"

*T*he criminal does not survive well.
The average criminal
spends the majority of his adult years
caged like some wild beast
and guarded from escape by the guns
of good marksmen.

Self Analysis

*T*he search for
and the attainment of pleasure
is not less valid in survival
than the avoidance of pain.

Dianetics: The Modern Science
of Mental Health

There is a necessity for pleasure,
a necessity as live and quivering
and vital as the human heart itself.
He who said that a man
who had two loaves of bread
should sell one to buy white hyacinth,
spoke sooth.
The creative, the constructive, the beautiful,
the harmonious, the adventurous, yes,
and even escape from the maw of oblivion:
these things are pleasure
and these things are necessity.

Dianetics: The Modern Science
of Mental Health

*An individual who can freely
and with a clear heart
do things because they're fun
is a very sane person.*

The Phoenix Lectures

*Rightness is conceived
to be survival. . . .
Theoretically, how right can one be?
Immortal!
How wrong can one be?
Dead!*

Scientology 8-8008

On
Goals

The basic formula of living (not life) is having and following a basic purpose.

Organization Executive Course:
"The Structure of Organization,
What Is Policy?"

The highest purpose in the universe is the creation of an effect.

Scientology: The Fundamentals of Thought

There is no totally easy way
to produce a desirable effect.
And the day you drop some of your ideas
of the effect you want to produce
is the day you get a little older,
a little weaker, a little less sane.

Organization Executive Course:
"Artistic Presentation"

*W*ithout goals, hopes,
ambitions or dreams,
   the attainment of pleasure
   is nearly impossible.

Science of Survival

*T*he goal is to win.
    When one has lost too much
and too many times,
    the possibility of winning
    seems too remote to try.

Self Analysis

*F*ailure consists exactly
    of something else happening
    rather than the intention.

A New Slant on Life

No man is happy without a goal,
and no man can be happy without faith
in his own ability to reach that goal.

Science of Survival

*D*reams, goals, ambitions—
these are the stuff
man uses for fuel.

Handbook for Preclears

There can be no purpose
worth contemplating
which does not include happiness
and experience.

When a man is no longer able
to envision happiness
as a part of his future,
that man is dead.

Dianetics 55!

54

*P*art of a goal
is its glamour
and part of any dream
is the man who dreamed it.

How to Live Though an Executive

*J*ust to have *something* to do
   and a *reason* to do it
      exerts a control over life itself.

If you have no purpose,
  you have no purchase on the small,
  first particle necessary
    to make the whole understandable.

Thus life can become a terrible burden.

The Problems of Work

If you act in the past,
you won't last.

The Route to Infinity Lectures:
Appendix, "Dianetics Jingles"

Future is the creation
of a future illusion
and the working toward that illusion
to make it a reality.

The Route to Infinity Lectures

*T*he essence of time is change.
Where there is no change
there is no time.

Dianetics 55!

*T*hose things which are scarce
are those things
which the individual
has lost his faith
in creating, in having.
An individual who cannot create
has to hold on to what he has.
This leads him into holding on to
what he has had.

The Creation of Human Ability

*I*magination could be classified
as the ability to create
or forecast a future
or to create, change or destroy
a present or past.

Scientology 8-8008

*A*ll the effort in the world
cannot overcome the idea
of one forthright man,
but a very small amount of thought
can make a slave
over a tremendous quantity
of emotion and effort.

Personal Achievement Series Lecture:
"Increasing Efficiency"

It is an interesting commentary upon the mental anatomy of man that he seldom intends to do something good without actually accomplishing something good.

A New Slant on Life

There is no more unhappy thing than a man who has accomplished all his ends in life.

Handbook for Preclears

Be true to your own goals.

The Creation of Human Ability

On
Happiness

*O*ften sought, but seldom found,
    there are no riches, gems or palaces
as valued as mere happiness.

Technical Bulletin:
"Clean Hands Make a Happy Life"

*A*ll the happiness you ever find
    lies in you.

A New Slant on Life

What has made all man a pauper
in his happiness?

*Transgressions against the mores of
his race,
his group,
his family!*

Technical Bulletin:
"Clean Hands Make a Happy Life"

Two rules for happy living:

1. *Be able to experience anything.*

2. *Cause only those things which others are able to experience easily.*

A New Slant on Life

*P*eople have value and are important.
Big or small
they are important.

Management Series: "Manners"

*Happiness and strength endure
only in the absence of hate.
To hate alone is the road to disaster.
To love is the road to strength.
To love in spite of all
  is the secret of greatness.
And may very well be
  the greatest secret
  in this universe.*

A New Slant on Life

*T*he ability to assume
　　　or to grant beingness
is probably the highest of human virtues.

Scientology: The Fundamentals of Thought

A person's importance
　　　is made evident to him
by showing him respect,
　　　or just by assuring him
he is visible and acceptable.

Management Series: "Manners"

It is even more important
to be able to permit other people
to have beingness
than to be able oneself to assume it.

Scientology: The Fundamentals of Thought

There is nothing wrong with being
the most important person under the sun
if everybody else is just
as important as you are.

The Hubbard Life Orientation Course

*The clue to happiness
is being interested in life.
People's happiness is as great
as they can create it.*

A New Slant on Life

*Happiness could be said to be
the overcoming
of not unknowable obstacles
toward a known
and desirable goal.*

Science of Survival

*H*appiness is power
and power is being able to do
what one is doing
when one is doing it.

Management Series: "Doing Work"

74

*T*o be happy,
one only must be **able** to confront,
which is to say, experience,
those things that are.

Unhappiness is only this:
the inability to confront
that which is.

A New Slant on Life

One who is plotting continually
how to get out of things
will be miserable.

One who is plotting
how to get into things
has a much better chance
of becoming happy.

Scientology: The Fundamentals of Thought

*There are various states of mind
    which bring about happiness.
That state of mind
    which insists only upon freedom
    can bring about nothing but unhappiness.
It would be better to develop
    a thought pattern
        which looked for new ways
            to be entrapped,
                and things to be trapped in,
        than to suffer
            the eventual total entrapment
                of dwelling upon freedom only.*

Scientology: The Fundamentals of Thought

*T*here is no need to lead a violent life
    just to prove one can experience.
The idea is not to prove
    one can experience,
        but to regain the **ability** to experience.

A New Slant on Life

*Happiness is not itself an emotion.
It is a word which states a condition
and the anatomy of that condition
is interest.*

A New Slant on Life

*The greatest joy there is in life
is creating.*

Splurge on it!

Technical Bulletin:
"The Joy of Creating"

On Production

Evidently there is no greater curse than total idleness.

Scientology: The Fundamentals of Thought

The common denominator of psychosis and neurosis is the inability to work.

The Phoenix Lectures

*P*roduction is the basis of morale.

Organization Executive Course:
"Morale"

The person who studiously avoids work
usually works far longer
and far harder
than the man who pleasantly
confronts it and does it.
Men who cannot work
are not happy men.

The Problems of Work

*To be denied the right to work
is to be denied
any part of the society
in which we live.*

The Problems of Work

*One can't be totally safe
in this universe.
But one can at least be effective!*

Organization Executive Course:
"Initiative"

Actually a "reward"
is what one desires,
not what is given.

Approval and validation
are often far more valuable
than material rewards
and are usually worked for
far harder than mere pay.

Organization Executive Course:
"Service"

There is ample reward
in the satisfaction of doing one's job
and being part of a self-respecting group.

Riches and power spring from that base.

Organization Executive Course:
"Initiative"

A man who cannot work
is as good as dead
and usually prefers death
and works to achieve it.

The Problems of Work

Morale
is dependent upon production.
Production is accomplished by
numerous contributions
of thought or effort.

Organization Executive Course:
"Service"

Outflow is holier,
more moral,
more remunerative
and more effective
than inflow.

Organization Executive Course:
"Outflow"

*A*ll slavery
is the consequence
of irresponsibility
and failure to do one's job.

Organization Executive Course:
"Initiative"

The rich man's son,
the moneyed dowager,
neither of them works.
Neither is sane.
When we look for neurosis
and folly in our society
we look toward those
who do not or cannot work.
When we look
over the background of a criminal
we look at "inability to work."

The Problems of Work

*M*en are not dispensable.
It is a mechanism of old philosophies
    to tell men
that if they think they are indispensable
    they should go down to the graveyard
        and take a look—
            those men were indispensable, too.

            This is the sheerest foolishness.

If you really looked carefully
   in the graveyard,
      you would find the machinist
who set the models going in yesteryear
   and without whom
      there would be no industry today.
         It is doubtful if such a feat
            is being performed just now.

The Problems of Work

All it is necessary to do to degrade or upset an individual is to prevent him from working.

The Problems of Work

*N*o *good worker owes his work.*
That's slavery.

Organization Executive Course:
"Rewards and Penalties, How to Handle
Personnel and Ethics Matters"

A workman is not just a workman.
A laborer is not just a laborer.
An office worker
is not just an office worker.
They are living, breathing,
important pillars
on which the entire structure
of our civilization is erected.
They are not cogs in a mighty machine.
They are the machine itself.

The Problems of Work

Somehow the right to work
seems to be bound up in happiness
and the zest of living.
And demonstrably
the denial of work
is bound up with madness
and insanity.

The Problems of Work

On
Leadership

*I*n all great leaders
    there is a purpose and intensity
which is unmistakable.
Plus there is a certain amount of courage
    required in a leader.

Management Series: "Leadership"

A man who merely wants to be liked
    will never be a leader.

Management Series: "Leadership"

*H*e who holds the power
of an organization
is that person
is that person
who holds its communication lines
and who is a crossroad
of the communications.

How to Live Though an Executive

*O*ne cannot hold power
and not use it.

Introduction to Scientology Ethics

*B*ad leadership
isn't "grouchy" or "sadistic"
or the many other things
man advertises it to be.
It is simply a leadership
that gives no or weak orders
and does not enforce compliance.

Management Series: "Leadership"

*P*eople are willing to do their best
and will
until hammered about it.

Organization Executive Course:
"Model Hat for an Executive"

Most people confuse a "taut ship"
with a harshly led ship.
Actually harshness
has nothing to do with it.
The right word is *positiveness*.

Management Series: "Leadership"

*The only capital an executive has
is the willingness to work.
Preserve it.
No person can be driven to labor—
as every slave society has found out.
They always lose.
When a man is whipped,
that work he then does still stems
from his willingness alone.
Anger made it smaller.*

Organization Executive Course:
"Model Hat for an Executive"

$\mathcal{A}$ good manager
takes care of the workers.
He also takes care of the organization.
A worker-oriented fellow—
union leader, agitator, do-gooder—
cares only for the worker
and thus does the worker in.

Management Series:
"Good Versus Bad Management"

If one would dream
  and see his dreams an actuality,
one must also be able to organize
  and to train organizational men
who will make those dreams come true.

Management Series:
"The Key Ingredients"

*Organizational genius is composed only
of arranging sequences of action
and designating channels
for types of particles.
That's all it is.*

Management Series:
"Cope and Organize"

*G*ood management carefully isolates
all stops on its flow lines
and eradicates them
to increase speed of flows.

Organization Executive Course:
"Speed of Service"

*R*eal help for the worker
is also making sure
there will be work for him to do.
When the organization is gone,
there is only misery, the dole,
revolution and sudden death.

Management Series:
"Good Versus Bad Management"

A common denominator
to all good executives
is the ability to communicate,
to have affinity for their area
and their people,
and to be able to achieve a reality
on existing circumstances.
All this adds up to understanding.
An executive who lacks
these qualities or abilities
is not likely to be very successful.

Management Series: "Leadership"

*I*gnore people at your peril.

Management Series: "Manners"

*You have no idea
how important people are.
There is a reversed ratio—
those at the bottom have a self-importance
far greater than those at the top
who are important.
A charlady's concept
of her own importance
is far greater than that
of a successful general manager!*

Management Series: "Manners"

The only thing that you ever object to
in important people
is that they act so thoroughly,
too many times,
on the supposition
that everybody else is a crumb.

The Hubbard Life Orientation Course

*A*sserting one's own importance
is about as acceptable
as a dead cat at a wedding.

Management Series: "Manners"

I believe that to command is to serve and only gives one the right to serve.

Organization Executive Course:
"Post, Handling Of"

Respect is a recognition of inspiration, purpose and competence and personal force or power.

Management Series: "Leadership"

On
Organizations

The purpose of organization is
to make planning
become actuality.

Management Series:
"The Key Ingredients"

The basic difference between organizations that run and those that collapse is simply somebody caring what happens to the organization itself.

Management Series:
"Good Versus Bad Management"

The most important zone of ethical conduct in an organization is at or near the top.

Management Series:
"Ethics and Executives"

No group can sit back
and expect its high brass
to be the only ones to carry the load.
The group is composed
of individual group members,
not of high brass.

Management Series:
"Environmental Control"

*I*ndividual initiative,
not orders,
makes a true group.

Organization Executive Course:
"Initiative"

The enturbulence
(commotion and upset)
in an organization
is directly proportional
to the ignorance or absence
of policy and purpose.

Organization Executive Course:
"Organizational Enturbulence"

The prosperity of any organization is directly proportional to the speed of its particles— goods, people, papers.

Organization Executive Course:
"Organization—The Flaw"

120

Anything which stops or delays the flows of a business or delays or puts a customer or product on **wait** *is an enemy of that business.*

Organization Execcutive Course:
"Speed of Service"

*If you reward nonproduction
you get nonproduction.
When you penalize production
you get nonproduction.
The welfare state can be defined
as that state
which rewards nonproduction
at the expense of production.*

Organization Executive Course:
"Rewards and Penalties,
How to Handle Personnel and Ethics Matters"

$\mathcal{J}$ustice is one of the guards
that keeps the channel of progress
a channel
and not a stopped flow.

Organization Executive Course:
"Administering Justice"

Emergencies don't just happen because someone is idle. Emergencies are made — actively.

Organization Executive Course:
"Danger Condition"

Orders only occur where responsibility has failed.

Organization Executive Course:
"Orders and Responsibility"

*Groups never seem to realize
that their hard times
are brought on by failures
in responsibility
and sharing the load.*

Organization Executive Course:
"Initiative"

*It is vital to any organization,
to be strong and effective,
to be ethical.*

Organization Executive Course:
"Ethics and Executives"

On
Society

A state has, as its sole assets,
the natural wealth of the state,
the willingness to work
on the part of its people
and the brightness of its thinkers.

Personal Achievement Series Lecture:
"The Road to Perfection,
The Goodness of Man"

*D*elete from a society
its willingness to participate
and its willingness to work,
and you've killed the society.

Personal Achievement Series Lecture:
"Man: Good or Evil"

*W*ork is only as good as it's enjoyed,
  not as it's paid.
Natural resources are only as good
  as they can be utilized,
    not thrown away.
And thought is only as good
  as it can express
    the goals and desires of man himself.
    And those things become wealth.

Personal Achievement Series Lecture:
"The Road to Perfection,
The Goodness of Man"

*The social ills of man
are chiefly a composite
of his personal difficulties.*

Technical Bulletin:
"Scientology Can Have a Group Win"

*A nation may have huge machines,
projectiles of great violence
and stoves that do all the cooking
and yet be a complete barbarism
socially.*

The Hubbard Life Orientation Course

$\mathcal{A}$ political system seeking to function
amongst ignorant, illiterate
and barbaric people
could have marvelous principles
but could only succeed in being ignorant,
illiterate and barbaric
unless one addressed the people
one by one and cured the ignorance,
illiteracy and barbarism
of each citizen.

Organization Executive Course:
"Politics"

131

*T*he barbarism solves political problems
with brutality,
crime with punishment
and social ills with degradation.

*Y*ou would not tolerate for one moment
the conduct in an individual
that is commonplace
in the acts of some nations.
You would lock up such a person.

$\mathcal{Y}$ou could define government
as "that body created
by the aggregate irresponsibility
of a people."

The Hubbard Life Orientation Course

*C*riminality and war
(and is there a difference?)
come about because of a staggering
social aberration.
This is only a composite
of individual aberrations.
People who believe otherwise
are just being irresponsible
for their share.

Technical Bulletin:
"Scientology Can Have a Group Win"

If you lump all the irresponsibility
in a nation
into one body
you would then have
an insane body.

Thus the government temper.

The Hubbard Life Orientation Course

Man *is basically good, yes.*
His experience has led him into evil
and he very often solves his problems
from his own point of view only.
And when he solves a problem
from his own point of view,
of course,
he gets other points of view
into trouble:
What is good for a duck hunter
is not good for the duck.

Filmed Interview: "An Introduction to Scientology"

*R*eason cannot be created
   or controlled by force.
Society exists
   because of persuading reason—
   or an agreement
      between reasonable beings.

Notes on the Lectures
of L. Ron Hubbard

*There is no national problem
in the world today,
    which cannot be resolved
    by reason alone.*

Dianetics: The Modern Science
of Mental Health

To cure a barbarism
one must make men
socially grow up.

And that is done with individuals.

*One works with individual people,
not with groups.*

The Hubbard Life Orientation Course

The only difference
in existing systems of politics
is their relative values
in giving the individual
a chance to develop
and receive a higher level
of personal sanity and ability.

Organization Executive Course:
"Politics"

A nation is as alive
as it has life in it.
It is as alive
as men are free to be.
It is as alive as men freely
support that nation toward its goals,
and it's no more alive
than that.

Personal Achievement Series Lecture:
"Health and Certainty"

On
Civilization

*I*deas and not battles
    mark the forward progress of mankind.
    Individuals, and not masses,
        form the culture of the race.

Science of Survival

*N*o sixteen-inch armor plate
could possibly stop an idea.

Dianetics 55!

*There is nothing wrong
with the world today,
except the world believes in duress
and slavery as a method of possession.*

Freedom Congress Lectures

All a suppressive person or society is trying to do is prevent one from flourishing and prospering.

Ron's Journal 31

*T*here is no argument on Earth
of sufficient emergency or violence
to require war,
much less war by atomic fission
with the consequence of the destruction
of at least one continent and,
within a few years,
the destruction of the planet Earth.

Dianetics 55!

*M*an's greatest weapon
is his reason.

Self Analysis

*T*he basic purpose of reason
is the calculation
or estimation of effort.

Advanced Procedure and Axioms

149

No war ever earned anything
but war.

Freedom Congress Lectures

*T*he ultimate weapon
is to flourish and prosper.

Ron's Journal 31

*M*an cannot afford slavery.
He cannot afford duress.
He can't afford to tear
his fellow man to pieces
if he wishes to live
any kind of a life at all.

Freedom Congress Lectures

*If the laws of tooth and claw
or self-preservation were basic laws,
there would be no one on Earth
at this time.*

Notes on the Lectures
of L. Ron Hubbard

Reasonably priced
and easily obtained justice
are requisites to any civilization.

Organization Executive Course:
"Chaplain's Court, Civil Hearings"

Any existing organization or civilization
is the sum total of its past
and current contributors
in terms of thought and effort.

Organization Executive Course:
"Service"

153

*The arts and skills of woman,
the creation and inspiration
of which she is capable and which—
here and there in isolated places
in our culture—she still manages to effect
in spite of the ruin and decay
of man's world
which spreads around her,
must be brought newly
and fully into life.
These arts and skills and creation
and inspiration are her beauty,
just as she is the beauty of mankind.*

Science of Survival

*There is no more deadly way
to get even with a suppressive
or an antagonistic person
or a downgrading society
than by flourishing and prospering.*

Ron's Journal 31

*One inherits tomorrow
what he died out of yesterday.*

The Problems of Work

On
Art

*A culture is only as great
as its dreams,
and its dreams are dreamed by artists.*

Science of Survival

A song can racket down the ages.
It doesn't corrode.
It doesn't have to be polished,
maintained, oiled, shelved
or put in a vault.
It happens that a song
is far more powerful
than any blaster ever invented.

The Philadelphia Doctorate Course Lectures

*S*uccessful works of art
have a message.
It may be implicit or implied,
emotional, conceptual or literal,
inferred or stated.
But a message nonetheless.

Technical Bulletin: "Message"

*A*rt is a word
which summarizes
the quality of communication.

Technical Bulletin: "Art"

Works of art are viewed by people.
They are heard by people.
They are felt by people.
They are not just the fodder
of a close-knit group of initiates.
They are the soul food of all people.

Technical Bulletin: "Art, More About"

Art is for the receiver.
If he understands it, he likes it.
If it confuses him
he may ignore or detest it.

Technical Bulletin: "Message"

Art seeks to create an effect.
An effect is not always
created the **easy** way.
Indeed, the better effects
are quite difficult to achieve.

Organization Executive Course:
"Artistic Presentation"

If you look at
　　　or listen to any work of art,
　there is only one thing
　　the casual audience
　　　responds to en masse,
　　　　and if this has it
　　　　　then you too will see it
　　　　　as a work of art.

　　　If it doesn't have it, you won't.

So what is it?

*Technical expertise itself adequate
to produce an emotional impact.*

*And that is how good
a work of art has to be
to be good.*

Technical Bulletin: "Art, More About"

*Seeking perfection
is a wrong target in art.
One should primarily
    seek communication with it
    and then perfect it
    as far as reasonable.
One attempts communication
    within the framework
    of applicable skill.
If perfection greater than that
    which can be attained
    for communication is sought,
    one will not communicate.*

Technical Bulletin: "Art"

It is not enough
that the creator of the work
understands it;
those who receive it must.

Technical Bulletin: "Message"

*L*iving itself is an art form.

Technical Bulletin: "Art, More About"

*The drive strength of the person
does not derive
from his aberrations.
The aberrations lessen the drive strength.
Artistry, personal force,
personality, all are residual
in the basic personality.*

The Dynamics of Life

"*Art for art's sake*"
is a complete paradox as a remark.
"Art for the sake of communication"
and "Attempted perfection
without communicating"
are the plus and minus of it all.

Technical Bulletin: "Art"

*A*rt takes that extra bit,
that extra care,
that bit more push
for it to be effective art.

Organization Executive Course:
"Artistic Presentation"

*I*t is actually pure balderdash
and a sort of a weak limping apology
for not being successful
to say that one works
for his own self-satisfaction.

Technical Bulletin: "How to View Art"

An artist stops his work
when he believes
he can no longer
create an effect.

Scientology: The Fundamentals of Thought

*S*ome people are themselves
a work of art
because they have mastered
the small practical techniques
of living
that give them a quality
adequate to produce
an emotional impact
even before anyone
knows their name
or what they do.

Technical Bulletin: "Art, More About"

The field of the arts
must be of all things
the most self-determined
of any of man's activities.

Lecture: "Attack on the Preclear"

It isn't magic or luck
that makes the professional.
It's hard won know-how
carefully applied.

Organization Executive Course:
"Artistic Presentation"

On
Being Cause

You should not minimize yourself as cause.
It is your greatest ability.

Organization Executive Course:
"Source to Cause"

The supreme test of a thetan is his ability to make things go right.

Organization Executive Course:
"The Supreme Test"

*Anything which you must not touch and upon which
you are not supposed to
have any effect at all
will sooner or later make you
the unwilling or unknowing
effect of it.*

Lecture: "Cause and Effect: Education,
Unknowing Effect"

People who explain how wrong
        it is all going
and who have reasons why and
        who aren't putting it right
are the real crazy people in the universe.
The only ones crazier than they are,
        are the ones who are quite happy
        to have everything fail
        and go wrong
                with no protest from them.

And the only ones even worse
are those who work endlessly
to make things go wrong
and prevent anything from going right
and oppose all efforts instinctively.
Fortunately there are a few around
who do make things go right
in spite of everything and anyone.

Organization Executive Course:
"The Supreme Test"

*W*hat is "hope"?
Hope is simply a future possibility that
    one might have an effect on something
    and is a substitute
      for being able
        to have it on something now.

Lecture: "Cause and Effect: Education,
Unknowing Effect"

*O*ne tries to be right **always**,
    right down to the last spark.

A New Slant on Life

*A*ll wrong actions
are the result of an error
followed by an insistence
on having been right.
Instead of righting the error
(which would involve being wrong)
one insists the error
was a right action
and so repeats it.

A New Slant on Life

*That man is selfish
is a valid statement
when one means an **aberrated** man.
That man is antisocial
is an equally valid statement
if one adds the modifier,
aberration.
And other such statements
resolve equally.*

Dianetics: The Modern Science
of Mental Health

*A fellow is a fool
if he thinks that he
can cause something
without becoming
one way or the other
the effect of it.*

The Phoenix Lectures

*B*laming something else
　　makes that something else cause;
and as that cause takes on power,
　　the individual in the same act
loses control and becomes effect.

Technical Bulletin:
"Cause and Effect"

*L*ife is not energy.
　　Energy is the byproduct of life.

Dianetics 55!

A thetan is interested,
and an object is interesting.
A thetan is not interesting.
He is interested.
And when a person
becomes terribly interesting
he has lots of problems,
believe me.

The Phoenix Lectures

*The passage from interested
to interesting has many phases.
When one is no longer interested,
but is only interesting,
he has lost his principle quality
as a thetan—
freedom,
and the ability
to change at will.*

The Creation of Human Ability

*B*ecause some people
cannot conceive
of **causing** anything,
they just watch it.
They don't **do** anything.
They are not **participants**.
They are spectators.

Organization Executive Course:
"Spectatorism"

When life becomes serious,
a man becomes less **cause** and greater **effect**.

Technical Bulletin:
"Cause and Effect"

*T*he basic difference
between aberration and sanity,
between inability and ability,
between illness and health,
is the knowingness
of causation by self
opposed to unknown causation
by others or other things.

Dianetics 55!

Being blamed
sometimes blunts being *cause*.
But if one's total ambition
is to be blameless,
the best situation
is to get one's name
on a tombstone.
And it's no fun being dead.

Organization Executive Course:
"Source to Cause"

On Morals and Ethics

*A*ll mankind lives
and each man strives
by codes of conduct
mutually agreed.
Perhaps these codes are good,
perhaps they're bad,
it's only evident they're codes.
Mores bind the race.

Technical Bulletin:
"Clean Hands Make a Happy Life"

The right of a person to survive is directly related to his honesty.

A New Slant on Life

Only the criminally inclined desire a society in which the criminal is free to do as he pleases.

Organization Executive Course:
"Administering Justice"

*There is nothing very glamorous
about the criminal,
    the breaker of his pledge,
        the betrayer of his friend or group.
Such people are simply psychotic.*

Science of Survival

*Only when he is beaten down
    below awareness as a chronic condition
does man commit evil actions.*

Technical Bulletin:
"Prediction and Consequences"

Individual rights were not originated
to protect criminals
but to bring freedom to honest men.
Into this area of protection
then dived those who needed "freedom"
and "individual liberty"
to cover their own
questionable activities.

A New Slant on Life

*The criminal accuses others
of things which he himself is doing.*

Technical Bulletin:
"The Criminal Mind"

*Only the criminally inclined
are frightened enough of justice
to protest and complain that it exists.*

Organization Executive Course:
"Administering Justice"

*U*nethical conduct
is actually the conduct
of destruction and fear;
lies are told
because one is afraid
of the consequences
should one tell the truth;
thus, the liar is inevitably a coward,
the coward is inevitably a liar.

Science of Survival

Man is basically good.
This is obvious.
For when he begins to do evil
he seeks to destroy his memory
in order to change
and seeks to destroy his body.
He seeks to check
his evil impulses
by inhibiting
his own skill and strength.

Technical Bulletin: "Psychosis"

To protect dishonest people
is to condemn them
to their own hells.

A New Slant on Life

A person who is dramatizing
his criminal intent
can become very angry
if he is not prevented
from hurting others.

Organization Executive Course:
"Administering Justice"

199

*It is not realized generally
that the criminal is not only antisocial
but is antiself.*

Science of Survival

*The criminal,
no matter what harm
he is doing to others,
is also seeking to destroy himself.
He is in protest
against his own survival.*

*Technical Bulletin:
"The Criminal Mind"*

Man's mortality,
his "one life" fixation,
all stem from his efforts
to check himself,
obliterate his memory
in a fruitless effort
to change his conduct
and his self-destructive habits
and impulses
and losses of skills and abilities.

Technical Bulletin: "Psychosis"

If a man uses his own honesty
to protest the unmasking of dishonesty,
then that man
is an enemy of his own freedom.

A New Slant on Life

*D*ecent people are in favor of justice.
Don't confuse the opinion
of the majority
who wish it
with the snarls of the few who fear it.

Organization Executive Course:
"Administering Justice"

$\mathcal{M}$an cannot be free
while there are those amongst him
who are slaves to their own terrors.

A New Slant on Life

*F*reedom is for honest people.
No man who is not himself honest
    can be free—
        he is his own trap.
When his own deeds
    cannot be disclosed,
        then he is a prisoner;
        he must withhold himself
        from his fellows
        and he is a slave
            to his own conscience.

A New Slant on Life

On Freedom

*T*he one impulse in man
which cannot be erased
is his impulse toward freedom,
his impulse toward sanity,
toward higher levels of attainment
in all of his endeavors.

Dianetics 55!

*Freedom for man
does not mean
freedom to injure man.
Freedom of speech
does not mean
freedom to harm by lies.*

*O*ne cannot go through life
victimizing one's fellow beings
and wind up in anything
but a trap—
the victim himself.

Technical Bulletin:
"The Anatomy of Failure"

*O*ne never observes
the forced individual
doing a job well,
just as one never observes
a forced society
winning against an
equally prosperous free society.

Dianetics: The Modern Science
of Mental Health

Freedom is
    the absence of barriers.
Less freedom is
    the presence of barriers.
    Entirely minus-freedom would be
        the omnipresence of barriers.
A barrier is matter or energy
    or time or space.
The more matter, energy, time and space
    assumes command over the individual
    the less freedom
    that individual has.

Dianetics 55!

Freedom from is all right
only so long as
there is a place to be free *to*.

An endless desire
for *freedom from*
is a perfect trap,
a fear of all things.

Scientology: The Fundamentals of Thought

Entrapment
    is the opposite of freedom.
A person who is not free
    is trapped.
He may be trapped by an idea,
    he may be trapped by matter,
        he may be trapped by energy,
            he may be trapped by space,
                he may be trapped by time,
    and he may be trapped
                by all of them.

Dianetics 55!

*F*ixed on too many barriers,
   man yearns to be free.
But launched into total freedom
   he is purposeless and miserable.
There is freedom among barriers.
If the barriers are known
   and the freedoms are known
      there can be life,
       living, happiness,
      a game.

Scientology: The Fundamentals of Thought

*F*reedom
　　　　depends on ability.

Organization Executive Course:
"Orders Versus Arbitraries"

*A*n unhappy man
is one who is considering
continually
how to become free.

Scientology: The Fundamentals of Thought

*There is no freedom
    in the absence of
affinity,
    agreement and
        communication.*

*Where an individual
    falls away from these
his freedom is sharply curtailed
    and he finds himself
confronted with
    barriers of magnitude.*

Dianetics 55!

A man who is willing
   to accept restrictions and barriers,
and is not afraid of them,
   is free.
A man who does nothing
   but fight restrictions and barriers
will usually be trapped.

Scientology: The Fundamentals of Thought

*D*eath itself
could be said
to be man's ultimate in entrapment.

When a man is totally entrapped
he is dead.

Dianetics 55!

A mind that is enslaved
is weak.
A mind that is free
is powerful,
and all the power there is,
is defined by and
contained in
freedom.

Dianetics 55!

It is a demonstrable law,
     not an opinion,
that he who would enslave his fellows
     becomes himself enslaved.

Handbook for Preclears

Each and every impulse of freedom
  is an impulse
     toward sanity,
      toward health,
       toward happiness.
  Every impulse toward slavery
    is an impulse in the direction of
    misery, disease and death.

Dianetics 55!

We must, however, assume,
   because it is so evident,
that an individual only gets into
   traps and circumstances
he intends to get into.

Certain it is that,
   having gotten into such a position,
he may be unwilling to remain in it,
   but a trap is always preceded by
one's own choice of entrance.

Scientology: The Fundamentals of Thought

If man cannot face what he is,
then man cannot be free.

Dianetics 55!

The only possible way
that you can get
any freedom
is to stop asking
everybody's permission
to be.

The Philadelphia Doctorate Course Lectures

On Games

Life is a game.
A game consists of *freedom,*
barriers
and purposes.

Scientology: The Fundamentals of Thought

*D*espite the amount of suffering,
pain, misery, sorrow and travail
which can exist in life,
the reason for existence
is the same reason
as one has to play a game—
interest, contest, activity
and possession.

Scientology: The Fundamentals of Thought

*Successes are little bits of living.
Failures are little bits of death.*

Handbook for Preclears

*Life has a motto
that any game
is better than no game.*

Dianetics 55!

It is quite obvious that if anyone
   controlled everything
      he would have no game.
There would be no unpredictable factors,
   no surprises in life.
   This might be said to be
a hell of considerable magnitude.

The Problems of Work

*The highest activity
is playing a game.*

A New Slant on Life

So eager is a thetan
    to have a game
that he will adopt to himself
    all manner of liabilities
      in order to have a parity
        with his opponents.
    One cannot have a game
with people who are too inferior
    in strength or cleverness.
Thus one reduces his own strength
    and cleverness
      in order to have a game.

The Creation of Human Ability

Truthfully, one never stops playing a game once started. He plays old games in secret— even from himself— while playing or not playing new ones. The only real game one can have is in present time. All others are in the past or in the future.

Dianetics 55!

*When an individual is not permitted
to be fully a part of the team
he is apt to choose
other members of the team
as his opponents
for, remember,
man must have a game.*

The Problems of Work

The game is the thing.
The wins and losses are not the thing.
One loses every time one wins,
for he then has no game.

The Creation of Human Ability

"Competition" is a trick of the weak to fetter the strong.

Organization Executive Course:
"Service"

The ideal state of being could be said to be wholly successful in all things.

*This is opposed
by being so unsuccessful
that one is dead.*

Handbook for Preclears

The game of life demands
that one assume a beingness
in order to accomplish
a doingness
in the direction
of havingness.

Scientology: The Fundamentals of Thought

An individual is not as alive
as his heart beats.
He is not as alive
as his toes wiggle.
No.
He is as live as
he can consent to play
the role he is playing.
If he is then playing that role
by his own consent,
he'll be alive to a remarkable degree.

Personal Achievement Series Lecture:
"Health and Certainty"

*Anything you shun
will have won.*

The Route to Infinity Lectures:
Appendix, "Dianetics Jingles"

On
Problems

Man

or any life form in this universe
seems to love problems.
A problem is more important
than freedom.
Problems keep up interest.

Scientology: The Fundamentals of Thought

Life poses problems
for its own solution.

The Creation of Human Ability

A problem consists
of two or more purposes opposed.
It does not matter what problem
you face or have faced,
the basic anatomy of that problem
is purpose–counter-purpose.

Scientology: The Fundamentals of Thought

When a man has a problem
very thoroughly
and can't solve it,
he really has too few problems.
He needs more.

Scientology: The Fundamentals of Thought

If we take a man
    and we keep giving him advice
    and giving him help
      and pushing him along and so on,
        we don't necessarily wind up with
        the resolution of his problems.
      But if, on the other hand,
      we put him in a position
        where he had higher intelligence,
        where his reaction time was better,

where he could confront life better,
where he could identify the factors
in his life more easily,
then he's in a position
where he can solve his own problems.
So he looks around,
he starts solving his own problems
and so he betters his own life.

Filmed Interview:
"An Introduction to Scientology"

Intelligence is the ability to perceive, pose and resolve problems.

Dianetics: The Modern Science
of Mental Health

*The insanity among the idle
is a matter of problem scarcity.*

Scientology: The Fundamentals of Thought

A thetan loves a problem.
And that is the basic of problems.

The Phoenix Lectures

If a person lacks problems,
    opponents and counter-purposes
        to his own,
            he will invent them.
        Here we have in essence
            the totality of aberration.

The Problems of Work

*Probably the problem
is the antidote to unconsciousness.
It is certainly the antidote for boredom.*

Scientology: The Fundamentals of Thought

*If you get somebody simply
to look around the environment,
he will cease to be a problem
and become the solver of problems.*

The Phoenix Lectures

*The real work here
is to put man in a mental condition
where he can solve his own problems.*

Filmed Interview:
"An Introduction to Scientology"

True sanity is that condition
   wherein one is sufficiently intelligent
    to solve his problems
       without physical violence
        or destroying other beings
   and yet survive happily and prosperously.

Technical Bulletin:
"Prediction and Consequences"

*T*o take apart a problem
requires only to establish
what one could not
or would not confront.

Organization Executive Course:
"Complexity and Confronting"

Man's difficulties
are a compound of his cowardices.
To have difficulties in life,
all it is necessary to do
is to start running away
from the business of livingness.
After that, problems of unsolvable
magnitude are assured.
When individuals are restrained
from confronting life,
they accrue a vast ability
to have difficulties with it.

A New Slant on Life

*The degree of complexity
is proportional
to the degree of nonconfront.*

Organization Executive Course:
"Complexity and Confronting"

*Anything which is not directly observed
tends to persist.*

The Creation of Human Ability

*A*ny problem,
to be a problem,
must contain a lie.

The Creation of Human Ability

On
Truth

You are an immortal soul.
Through lies, treachery,
   deceit and pretense
      you can destroy yourself.
By seeking truth
and living a life of helping others,
   by being honest and decent
you will be strong and achieve
      your power and immortality.

Article: "The Meaning of Scientology"

*Truth is actually a relative quantity;
it could be said to be
the most reasonable existing data
about any body of facts.*

Science of Survival

A thing to be "good"
would depend on
the viewpoint of the observer,
and the same condition
would exist for "bad."

Scientology 8-8008

Goodness and badness,
beautifulness and ugliness
are alike considerations
and have no other basis than opinion.

The Creation of Human Ability

What is true for you
is what you have observed yourself.

And when you lose
that you have lost everything.

Technical Bulletin:
"Personal Integrity"

Truth,
as a manifestation of human conduct,
would be the holding or voicing
of facts as one knows them
and refusal to utter or hold statements
contrary to what one knows.

Science of Survival

*There is no liar
lying like an angry man.*

The Phoenix Lectures

*Truth is built by those who have
the breadth and balance
to see also where they're wrong.*

A New Slant on Life

*K*nowledge, truth, secrets—
they are the guts and anatomy of life.
They must not then be owned.
They must not then be hidden or bent.
They must be permitted to stand out
in the bold sunlight for all to see,
for only when they are to be seen
are they safe things to have,
to hold, to know.

Dianetics 55!

*A body of knowledge
cannot have an **opinion** on something;
it simply extends
what is found to be true
wherever it is found to be true
into greater truths.*

The Phoenix Lectures

Truth is not determined by its appeal but by the evidence.

Article: (Untitled)

If you get caught in the middle, it's because you've bought a riddle.

The Route to Infinity Lectures:
Appendix, "Dianetics Jingles"

*I*t could be said that life
was made to be lived,
not died out of;
and that facts
which encourage a high level of living
would be, for man,
the most truthful facts;
and that those which encourage
his demise
would be the most untruthful facts.

Science of Survival

*In the final analysis
all you can get anybody to do
is inspect himself, his environment,
life, and find out what's true for him.*

Personal Achievement Series Lecture:
"Differences Between Scientology and
Other Studies"

*I know no man who has any monopoly
upon the wisdom of this universe.
It belongs to those who **can** use it
to help themselves and others.*

Article: "My Philosophy"

On Data and Knowledge

$\mathcal{K}$*nowledge is*
a total certainty and
understanding of data
and this can include
objects, actions, spaces
or areas, time and forms.

Technical Bulletin:
"Knowledge, Definition Of"

*Intelligence and judgment
are measured by
the ability to
evaluate relative importances.*

The Creation of Human Ability

*Any information
is valuable to the degree
that you can use it.*

Scientology: The Fundamentals of Thought

$\mathcal{D}$ata is something one uses
to think with.
It isn't thinking.
And when the data
becomes a substitute for thinking
we have frozen
the whole forward progress
of education.

Lecture: "Cause and Effect: Education,
Unknowing Effect"

*Insecurity exists
in the absence of knowledge.
All security
derives from knowledge.*

The Problems of Work

$\mathcal{T}$o the degree
that a being cannot confront,
he enters substitutes which,
accumulating,
bring about a complexity.

Organization Executive Course:
"Complexity and Confronting"

280

We expect
the fundamentals of behavior
to be complicated simply because
so many highly complicated people
have discussed the subject.

Dianetics 55!

*Creativeness could be found
to exceed existence itself;
by observation and definition
it is discoverable that thought
does not necessarily have to
be preceded by data,
but can create data.*

Scientology 8-8008

All answers are basically simple.

Dianetics: The Evolution of a Science

*The degree of simplicity
is proportional to
the degree of confront.*

Organization Executive Course:
"Complexity and Confronting"

The wise man tests before he talks.
The critic but follows the fad
of a cynical and apathetic age.

Self Analysis

*W*isdom is not a fixed idea.
It is knowing how to use your wits.

Management Series:
"Narrowing the Target"

*The need for all discipline
can be traced back to
the inability to think.
Even when appearing clever,
criminals are idiots;
they have not ever thought
the thought through.*

Management Series:
"The Anatomy of Thought"

The criminal is ignorant and stupid. Ignorance and stupidity may therefore be called criminal.

Scientology: The Fundamentals of Thought

It could be said with some truth that the person who asserts he needs to know no more to be fully as bright as his fellows, would, upon examination, be discovered to be quite deficient in capability and understanding.

Dianetics 55!

One can always know
   something about anything.
It is a wise man who,
   confronted with conflicting data,
realizes that he knows
   at least one thing
      —that he doesn't know.

Management Series: "Logic"

*Actually, a snapping bright mind
and an alert body are worth
a hundred thousand years of "experience"
behind some dusty desk or counter,
and an ability to do a "quick study"
of a subject is so much more valuable
than an education—complete with
a hundred A's—in that subject that one
might be led to suppose that maybe
"education," as it is laughingly called,
might possibly be overstressed.*

Check your history and you will discover
that the men whose marble busts adorn
the modern halls of learning did not
themselves have a formal education:
Bacon, Spencer, Voltaire, etc., etc., etc.,
down the whole list;
two or three exceptions prove the rule.

Handbook for Preclears

On
Certainty

*K*nowledge itself is certainty;
knowledge is not data.

A New Slant on Life

The greatest ability of thought
is differentiation.
So long as one can differentiate,
one is sane.
Its opposite is identification.

A New Slant on Life

*T*he ability to think has to do with
the ability to differentiate.
Unthinkingness has to do with
a lack of ability to differentiate
and a compulsion to identify unlike things
with each other
as though they were not only like things
but the same thing.

Science of Survival

294

*T*o obtain a certainty
one must be able to observe.

A New Slant on Life

*P*eople at low levels of awareness
do not observe,
but substitute for observation
preconceptions, evaluation and
suppositions, and even physical pain
by which to attain their certainties.

The Creation of Human Ability

*T*he social order has confused
 irrationality with emotionalism.
Actually
 a person who is fully rational
would be most able to respond
 to the stimulus of his environment.
Being rational does not mean
 being cold and calculating.

Self Analysis

*K*nowledge does not destroy
a will to live.
Pain and loss of self-determinism
destroy that will.

Self Analysis

A confusion can be defined
as any set of factors or circumstances
which do not seem to have
any immediate solution.
More broadly,
a confusion in this universe
is random motion.

The Problems of Work

A confusion
is only a confusion
so long as **all** particles
are in motion.
A confusion
is only a confusion
so long as
no factor is clearly defined
or understood.

The Problems of Work

*C*onfusion
is the basic cause of stupidity.

The Problems of Work

*U*ntil one selects
one datum, one factor, one particular
in a confusion of particles,
the confusion continues.
The one thing selected and used
becomes the stable datum
for the remainder.

The Problems of Work

A stable datum is necessary
to the alignment of data.

The Creation of Human Ability

*W*hen we grow timid
in the face of circumstance
it is because our purpose,
our stable data,
have been invalidated.

The Problems of Work

*I*t is a truism
that youth thinks fast
on little experience.
And that age thinks slowly
on much.

Self Analysis

*C*ertainty, then,
　　is clarity of observation.
Of course, above this,
　　vitally so,
is certainty in creation.
　　　Here is the artist,
　　here is the master,
　　here is the very great spirit.

A New Slant on Life

On
Sanity

*Sanity is certainty,
    providing only that
that certainty does not fall beyond
    the conviction of another
when he views it.*

A New Slant on Life

Sanity is the ability to recognize differences, similarities and identities.

Management Series:
"The Anatomy of Thought"

Sanity and insanity
are matters of motive,
not rationality or competence.
The sane are constructive,
the insane are destructive.

Organization Executive Course:
"Valuable Final Products"

*The basic thing man
can't or won't confront
is evil.*

Organization Executive Course:
"Complexity and Confronting"

*Insanity is the overt or covert
but always complex and continuous
determination to harm or destroy.*

Technical Bulletin: "Psychosis"

$\mathcal{M}$an is not trying to do evil.
   He isn't a suppressed being.
He's a being that's been fighting
   the mysterious, the supernatural,
the superstitious, the evil in life,
   and losing too often.
And where he loses,
   you get the criminal.
You get the insane.

Personal Achievement Series Lecture:
"Miracles"

Now it is a fact
that help and destroy
are opposite ends
of the same string.
When a person can no longer help
he seeks to destroy.

The Hubbard Life Orientation Course

You can't beat a man into sanity.

Science of Survival

The road from insanity
to sanity is a road of recognition
of the world around one,
the future and consequences
of one's own actions.

Technical Bulletin:
"Prediction and Consequences"

If you want to be tall, just be all.

The Route to Infinity Lectures:
Appendix, "Dianetics Jingles"

The modern trend of "don't do"
accompanies the modern trend
of an increased percentage of the insane
in the society.

The crazier a person is,
the less he accomplishes or does.

So we live in a world which is
oriented to drive men mad.

Organization Executive Course:
"Artistic Presentation"

*The insane are irresponsible.
That is why they are insane.*

The Hubbard Life Orientation Course

*Decision is sanity
and indecision is aberration.*

The Route to Infinity Lectures

*The one fear
the psychotic has
is becoming
predictable.*

Dianetics 55!

*When men become too confused
to even stay in the present,
they slide into the past
and become "psychotic"
or, at best, "neurotic."*

Technical Bulletin:
"Prediction and Consequences"

There is a basic rule that
    a psychotic person is
        concerned with the
        past,
    a neurotic person is barely
        able to keep up
        with the present
    and a sane person is
        concerned with the future.

A New Slant on Life

*I*nsanity is contagious.
Confusion is contagious.
Have you ever talked
to a confused man
without yourself,
at the end of the conversation,
feeling a little confused?

The Problems of Work

A sane man has difficulty in insane surroundings.

The Problems of Work

The road to sanity is demonstrably the road to increasing certainty.

A New Slant on Life

On
Control

*Control is the ability
and willingness to start,
change or stop something at will
or determine its fate or future.*

The New Hubbard Professional TR Course

A confusion could be called
an *uncontrolled randomness.*
Only those who can exert some control
over that randomness
can handle confusions.
Those who cannot exert control
actually breed confusions.

The Problems of Work

The anatomy of control is
start,
change
and stop.

Scientology: The Fundamentals of Thought

There could be three things wrong with any person, and these would be the inability to start, the inability to change, the inability to stop.

Scientology: The Fundamentals of Thought

*The only way a mind can be controlled
is by enforcing upon it
ignorance of itself.*

Dianetics 55!

*P*eople who are able
to control something
do not need to be afraid of it,
and do not suffer
ill effects from it.
People who cannot control things
can receive bad effects
from those things.

Dianetics 55!

*T*he secret of doing a good job
is the secret of control itself.
One not only continues
to create a job, day by day,
week by week, month by month,
he also continues the job
by permitting it to progress,
and he is also capable of stopping
or ending any cycle of work
and letting it remain finished.

The Problems of Work

*The individual who absolutely
has to control everything in sight
is upsetting to all of us
and this individual
is why we have begun
to find things wrong with control.*

The Problems of Work

Actually, one is done wrong
by the weaklings of this world,
not by the strong men.
One does not have to enslave
and control by force
those whose conduct he does not fear.
When you find an individual
who is bent entirely
upon a course of the arduous control
of the motions of others,
you are looking at an individual
who is afraid.
By their fear you shall know them.

Dianetics 55!

*I*f your mest is in disorder,
   your case is on the border.

If your mest is in good shape,
   you haven't time to hate.

The Route to Infinity Lectures:
Appendix, "Dianetics Jingles"

*O*ne's "standards"
(the degree of rightness one is trying
to establish and maintain)
are directly related to one's desire
to have a controlled environment.

Management Series:
"Environmental Control"

*T*here is *good* control and **bad** control.
The difference between them
is certainty and uncertainty.
Good control is certain,
positive, predictable.
Bad control is uncertain,
variable and unpredictable.

The Problems of Work

*The attainment of one's **standards**
is not done by criticism
(a human system).
It is done by exerting control
of one's environment
and moving things effectively
toward a more ideal scene.*

Management Series:
"Environmental Control"

*One's health and ability
rise directly as one asserts
greater and surer control
over his surroundings.*

Handbook for Preclears

On
Ability

*A*bility is demonstrated
by the handling of
matter, energy, space and time.

Dianetics 55!

The easiest thing a thetan does is change his mind. The most difficult thing he does is handle the environment in which he finds himself situated.

Scientology: The Fundamentals of Thought

An individual is as well off
as he can change things
in location in space.

The Phoenix Lectures

*E*very extinct species became extinct
because it could not change
to control a new environment.

Self Analysis

A man is as sane
as he is dangerous to the environment.
What occurs is that the environment
becomes dangerous to the man
and the man cannot be dangerous
to the environment.
And his answer to this
is immobility
and general deterioration.

The Creation of Human Ability

*Just because it made you fall
doesn't prove that it is all.*

The Route to Infinity Lectures:
Appendix, "Dianetics Jingles"

We live in a machine world.
The whole yap
of television and newspapers
is directed toward reducing effort.
The primary goal of the civilization
in which we live, it seems,
is to reduce all personal effort to zero.

Organization Executive Course:
"Artistic Presentation"

There is a direct ratio between
the health and ability of the person
and his willingness to accept responsibility.

The Phoenix Lectures

*W*hile all men are created
with equal rights under the law,
an examination of the individuals
in the society rapidly demonstrates
that all men are not created
with equal potential value
to their fellows.

Science of Survival

*Y*our potentialities
are a great deal better
than anyone ever permitted
you to believe.

Self Analysis

*I*t's impossible to reduce an ability.
About the only thing you can do
is reduce its exercise
or the willingness to exercise it.

Lecture: "Control"

*T*he less effort a being can confront,
the more effect of effort he becomes.

Organization Executive Course:
"Artistic Presentation"

*Competence is not a question
of one being
being more clever than another.
It is one being
being more able
to do what he is doing
than another is.*

Management Series: "Doing Work"

348

*W*hen a person is competent,
nothing can shake his pride.
The world can yell.
But it doesn't shake him.

Management Series: "Doing Work"

*Ability is dependent entirely
upon a greater
and better understanding
of that field or area
in which one cares
to be more able.*

Dianetics 55!

*The highest form of security
is confidence in one's self
in the future,
in the group
and in mankind.*

Science of Survival

*Self-confidence alone is security.
Your ability is your security.
There is no security but you.*

Handbook for Preclears

On Handling Situations

*The first step
of handling anything
is gaining an ability
to face it.*

A New Slant on Life

That which one cannot accept chains one.

The Creation of Human Ability

It is a truism that one never solves
anything by running away from it.
Of course, one might also say
that one never solves cannonballs
by baring his breast to them.
But I assure you that if nobody cared
whether cannonballs were fired or not,
control of people by threat of cannonballs
would cease.

A New Slant on Life

*I*f all things you would flee,
these you'll be.

The Route to Infinity Lectures:
Appendix, "Dianetics Jingles"

*I*f one knows the tech
of how to do something
and can do it, and uses it,
he cannot be the adverse effect of it.

Organization Executive Course:
"Your Post and Life"

The way out is the way through.

The Creation of Human Ability

*Things do not run right
because one is holy or good.
Things run right
because one makes them run right.*

Introduction to Scientology Ethics

*I*f you don't want to be attacked
don't draw back.

The Route to Infinity Lectures:
Appendix, "Dianetics Jingles"

*T*hat which a person withdraws from
in this universe becomes,
to a marked degree, his master.

Dianetics 55!

*P*eople are the victims
of their own flinch.
They are the victims
of their own postulates,
the victims of their own belief
that they are inadequate.

A New Slant on Life

$\mathcal{T}$hat which one fears,
one becomes.

Dianetics 55!

*N*ow, it is very, very true that man has a very definite alignment with this law: That which you resist you become. There's another little clause that belongs on the bottom of it: if you lose.

Personal Achievement Series Lecture: "Miracles"

*T*he basis of aberration
is a nonconfront.

Organization Executive Course:
"Complexity and Confronting"

*T*hat which a person can confront,
he can handle.

A New Slant on Life

Responsibility is the nonrecognition
and denial of the right of intervention
between oneself and any being,
idea, matter, energy, space, time or form,
and the assumption of full right of
determination over it.

The New Hubbard Professional TR Course

$\mathcal{T}$he only trap
into which life can fall
is to do things
without knowing it is doing them.

Dianetics 55!

The wrong thing to do
about any given circumstance
or situation
is to do nothing.

The Hubbard Life Orientation Course

If you act in today
you keep morrow away.

The Route to Infinity Lectures:
Appendix, "Dianetics Jingles"

The only time anyone
has ever gotten
into serious trouble
was when he decided
he could do nothing
about something.

Dianetics 55!

On
Self

The only aberration
is denial of self.
Nobody else can do
anything to you
but you.

A New Slant on Life

*You are treating yourself
    in present time
much as you were treated by others
    in the past.
And you punish yourself far more than
    anyone would ever punish you.*

Handbook for Preclears

*A*ctually,
   you are a giant
tied down with cotton lint.
You tied the knots
and furnished the string
   and said where you'd lie.

Handbook for Preclears

The individual
is not his analytical mind,
he is not his reactive mind,
he is not his body
any more than
he is his house or his car.

Dianetics 55!

Anything you can see,
you can be.

The Route to Infinity Lectures:
Appendix, "Dianetics Jingles"

In the opinion of the viewpoint,
    any beingness, any thing, is better
      than no thing,
    any effect is better than no effect,
    any universe better than no universe,
    any particle better than no particle,
    but the particle of admiration
      is best of all.

The Creation of Human Ability

Probably the most
neglected friend you have
is you.

Self Analysis

A healthy state of being
is to be a friend to yourself.
If you have few friends,
if you don't like friends,
you won't like yourself either.

Handbook for Preclears

*O*ne is what one is,
not what one is
admired or hated for.

Introduction to Scientology Ethics

*T*he basic individual
is not a buried unknown
or a different person,
but an intensity of all that is
best and most able
in the person.

The Dynamics of Life

It will be discovered
that most individuals
are involved with fighting
themselves.

The Creation of Human Ability

377

*T*here is beingness,
    but man believes
there is only becomingness.

The Creation of Human Ability

*Y*our ideas about yourself
    really don't monitor your behavior at all.
But your ideas about the other fellow
    monitor your behavior.

Personal Achievement Series Lecture:
"Man's Relentless Search"

$\mathcal{T}$he only reason
　　　some people find ambition
is a spike
　　　　is they don't try to be,
　　　　　　they try to be like.

The Route to Infinity Lectures:
Appendix, "Dianetics Jingles"

*Self-confidence
is nothing more than
belief in
one's ability to decide
and in
one's decisions.*

Handbook for Preclears

*J*ust as you do not want
    people to control you,
so you should want
    knowledge of yourself and others.
Just as you fight away
    from knowingness concerning self,
so you will be controlled.

Dianetics 55!

*Self-invalidation is merely
the accumulation of invalidation
of oneself
by others.*

Organization Executive Course:
"Ethics Presence"

You make New Year's resolutions.

And you make them
    into the teeth of old resolutions
which were different.

Then you don't keep
    your new resolutions
and you tell yourself
    you are weak-willed.

You aren't weak-willed,
    you are simply obeying yourself
as of yesterday.

Handbook for Preclears

*Never disparage yourself
or
minimize your strength
or power.*

The Creation of Human Ability

*The power of a thetan
stems from his ability
to hold a position in space.*

Management Series: "Why Hatting?"

Never regret yesterday.
Life is in you today,
and you make your tomorrow.

The Creation of Human Ability

On
Man

*M*an is not a reactive animal.
　　He is capable of self-determinism.
　　He has willpower.

The Dynamics of Life

$\mathcal{M}$an is basically good.
Pain and
social aberrations
turn him away from
high ethics, efficiency
and happiness.

Self Analysis

*M*ost people are not emotional—
they are misemotional,
in that they do not react
to the situations in their environment
with the emotion which would be
most rational to display.

Self Analysis

*It is a rather noble commentary on man
that when a person finds himself,
as he believes,
incapable of restraining himself
from injuring a benefactor
he will defend the benefactor
by leaving.*

Technical Bulletin: "Blow-Offs"

*M*an succeeds because
he adjusts his environment to *him*,
not by adjusting himself
to the environment.

Self Analysis

*W*herever man strives,
wherever he works,
whatever he does,
the good he does
outweighs the evil.

Personal Achievement Series Lecture:
"Miracles"

*The individual himself
is a spirit
controlling a body
via a mind.*

Scientology: The Fundamentals of Thought

A man is his own immortal soul.

A New Slant on Life

*You ask somebody,
"What is a spirit,"
and you might as well ask,
"How are you?"*

Filmed Interview:
"An Introduction to Scientology"

The soul is life,
 is the spirit,
  is the thinkingness,
  is the awareness
 or any such term
  which communicates to you
  the meaning of
  life and vitality.

Personal Achievement Series Lecture:
"Man: Good or Evil"

Life itself does not die.
Only the physical organism dies.
Not even a personality, apparently, dies.
Death then, in truth,
is a limited concept
of the death of the physical part
of the organism.
Life and the personality,
apparently, go on.
The physical part of the organism
ceases to function.
And that is death.

Self Analysis

*An individual
becomes aberrated
by additives.*

Technical Bulletin:
"Recognition of Rightness of the Being"

*Without free emotion,
an individual cannot appreciate
as he should
the pleasant things
in his environment.*

Self Analysis

397

Man can only become a machine
when he is no longer capable
of understanding his own beingness
and has lost his contact with it.

Dianetics 55!

An individual is basically
and routinely good,
capable of many actions
and considerable power.

Technical Bulletin:
"Recognition of Rightness of the Being"

$\mathcal{P}$eople
who cannot experience emotion
because of their aberrations
are ordinarily sick people.
Well people
can experience emotion.

Self Analysis

$\mathcal{M}$an is an added-to being
and everything
that has been added to him
has decreased his ability to cope.
When you add something
to the being
he gets worse.

Technical Bulletin:
"Recognition of Rightness of the Being"

*M*an has been invalidated
to such an extent
that he starts to do himself in—
that's the secret of aberration.

Organization Executive Course:
"Ethics Presence"

On
Children

When children become unimportant
to a society,
that society has forfeited
its future.

Science of Survival

*C*hildren are not dogs.
They can't be trained
like dogs are trained.
They are not controllable items.
They are, and let's not
overlook the point,
men and women.

A New Slant on Life

*Children, in the main,
are quite willing
to work.*

The Problems of Work

A child is not a special
species of animal
distinct from man.
A child is a man or a woman
who has not attained full growth.

A New Slant on Life

*T*he adult is the problem
in child raising,
not the child.

Child Dianetics

"*My child,*"
is often the parent's fond manner
of alluding to his offspring.
But that isn't "my child."
That is Bobby—
a person in his own right.

Technical Bulletin: "Mest Processing"

A good, stable adult
with love and tolerance in his heart
is about the best therapy a child can have.

Child Dianetics

*I*t is a remarkable fact,
a scientific fact,
that the healthiest children
come from the happiest mothers.

Dianetics: The Modern Science
of Mental Health

*Forbidding children to work,
and particularly forbidding teenagers
to make their own way in the world
and earn their own money,
creates a family difficulty
so that it becomes almost impossible
to raise a family,
and creates as well, and particularly,
a state of mind in the teenager
that the world does not want him,
and he has already lost his game
before he has begun it.*

The Problems of Work

*The spoiled child
is the child whose decisions
have been interrupted continuously
and who is robbed of his independence.*

Dianetics: The Modern Science
of Mental Health

*You've lost the child forever
that you seek to control and own.*

Child Dianetics

*The basic difficulty
with all juvenile delinquency
is the one-time apparently
humane program
of forbidding children
to labor in any way.*

The Problems of Work

413

*Y*ou want to raise your child
      in such a way
that you don't have to control him,
so that he will be in full possession
      of himself at all times.
Upon that depends his good behavior,
      his health, his sanity.

Child Dianetics

Affection could no more spoil a child than the sun could be put out by a bucket of gasoline.

Dianetics: The Modern Science of Mental Health

On
Human
Relationships

The hardest task one can have
is to continue to love his fellows
despite all reasons he should not.

And the true sign
of sanity and greatness
is to so continue.

A New Slant on Life

*In a culture,
manners are the lubrication
that ease the frictions
of social contacts.*

Technical Bulletin: "Stage Manners"

*A primary trap
is to succumb to
invitations to hate.*

A New Slant on Life

419

*There are no conflicts
which cannot be resolved
unless the true promoters of them
remain hidden.*

A New Slant on Life

While it is commonly believed to take two to make a fight, a third party must exist and must develop it for actual conflict to occur.

A New Slant on Life

You have heard
some very absurd arguments
out among the crowd.
Realize that the speaker
was more interested in
asserting his or her own rightness
than in being right.

A New Slant on Life

*The always last sung song,
"I was wrong."*

The Route to Infinity Lectures:
Appendix, "Dianetics Jingles"

*We have long said that
that which is not admired
tends to persist.
If no one admires
a person for being right,
then that person's
"brand of being right"
will persist, no matter how
mad it sounds.*

A New Slant on Life

Ridicule
  is the very lightest method
  of just slapping you to pieces.

The Phoenix Lectures

True greatness merely refuses to change
in the face of bad actions against one—
          and a truly great person
              loves his fellows
      because he understands them.

A New Slant on Life

A human being
feels able and competent
only so long as
he is permitted to contribute
as much as or more than
he has contributed to him.

A New Slant on Life

426

A welfare state
requiring no contribution
will at length
be paid in revolution.

Organization Executive Course:
"Service"

$\mathcal{R}$ewards
are not necessarily proportional
to contribution
and do not necessarily
establish the degree
of contribution.

Organization Executive Course:
"Service"

*H*e who would give
      must be willing to receive.
He who would receive
      must be willing to give.

Scientology: The Fundamentals of Thought

*M*y own philosophy
is that one should
share what wisdom he has,
one should help others
to help themselves,
and one should keep going
despite heavy weather
for there is always a calm ahead.

Article: "My Philosophy"

*O*n the day
when we can fully trust each other,
there will be peace on Earth.

A New Slant on Life

About the Author

About the Author

L. Ron Hubbard is one of the most acclaimed and widely read authors of all time, primarily because his works express a firsthand knowledge of the nature of man—knowledge gained not from standing on the sidelines but through lifelong experience with people from all walks of life.

As Ron said, "One doesn't learn about life by sitting in an ivory tower, thinking about it. One learns about life by being part of it." And that is how he lived.

He began his quest for knowledge on the nature of man at a very early age. When he was eight years old he was already well on his way to being a seasoned traveler. His adventures included voyages to China, Japan and other points in the Orient and South Pacific, covering a quarter of a million miles by the age of nineteen. In the course of his travels he became closely acquainted with twenty-one different races and cultures all over the world.

In the fall of 1930, Ron pursued his studies of mathematics and engineering, enrolling at George Washington University where he was also a member of one of the first American classes on nuclear physics. He realized that neither the East nor the West contained the full answer to the problems of existence. Despite all of mankind's advances in the physical sciences, a *workable* technology of the mind and life had never been developed. The mental "technologies" which did exist, psychology and psychiatry, were actually barbaric, false subjects—no more workable than the methods of jungle witch doctors. Ron shouldered the responsibility of filling this gap in the knowledge of mankind.

He financed his early research through fiction writing. He became one of the most highly demanded authors in the golden age of popular adventure and science fiction writing during the 1930s and 1940s, interrupted only by his service in the US Navy during World War II.

Partially disabled at the war's end, Ron applied what he had learned from his researches. He made breakthroughs and developed techniques which made it possible for him to recover from his injuries and help others to regain their health. It was during this time that the basic tenets of Dianetics technology were codified.

In late 1947, he wrote a manuscript detailing his discoveries. It was not published at that time, but circulated amongst Ron's friends, who copied it and passed it on to others. (This manuscript was formally published in 1951 as *Dianetics: The Original Thesis* and later republished as *The Dynamics of Life*.) The interest generated by this manuscript prompted a flood of requests for more information on the subject.

Ron provided all his discoveries to the American Psychiatric Association and the American Medical Association. Despite the fact that his work would have benefited them and society immensely, they ignored his research and continued on with their archaic activities.

Meanwhile, the steadily increasing flow of letters asking for further information and requesting that he detail more applications of his new subject resulted in Ron spending all his time answering letters. He decided to write and publish a comprehensive text on the subject— *Dianetics: The Modern Science of Mental Health.*

With the release of *Dianetics* on 9 May 1950, a complete handbook for the application of Ron's new technology was broadly available for the first time. Public interest spread like wildfire. The book shot to the top of the *New York Times* bestseller list and remained there week after week. More than 750 Dianetics study groups sprang up within a few months of its publication.

Ron's work did not stop with the success of *Dianetics* but accelerated, with new discoveries and breakthroughs a constant, normal occurrence. In his further research he discovered the very nature of life itself and its exact relationship to this universe. These discoveries led to his development of Scientology, the first workable technology for the improvement of conditions in any aspect of life. Scientology encompasses techniques which can help increase a person's success in his own personal relationships, at his work and in his day-to-day activities.

Through the 1960s, 70s and into the 80s, Ron continued his research and writing, amassing an enormous volume of material totaling over 60 million words—recorded in books, manuscripts and taped lectures. Today these works are studied and applied daily in hundreds of Scientology churches, missions and organizations around the world.

With his research fully completed and codified, L. Ron Hubbard departed his body on 24 January 1986.

Ron's work opened a wide bridge to understanding and freedom for mankind. Through his efforts, there now exists a totally workable technology with which people can help each other improve their lives and succeed in achieving their goals.

Glossary

aberration: a departure from rational thought or behavior. Aberration means basically to err, to make mistakes, or more specifically to have fixed ideas which are not true. The word is also used in its scientific sense. It means departure from a straight line. If a line should go from A to B, then if it is *aberrated* it would go from A to some other point, to some other point, to some other point, to some other point, to some other point, and finally arrive at B. Taken in its scientific sense, it would also mean the lack of straightness or to see crookedly as, for example, a man sees a horse but thinks he sees an elephant. Aberrated conduct would be wrong conduct, or conduct not supported by reason. Aberration is opposed to sanity, which would be its opposite. From the Latin, *aberrare*, to wander from; Latin, *ab*, away, *errare*, to wander. *Criminality and war (and is there a difference?) come about because of a staggering social aberration. This is only a composite of individual aberrations.*

Ability: the magazine of the Founding Church of Scientology of Washington, DC, since 1955. *[Bibliography: Personal Integrity,* Ability *125, Feb. 61]*

accrue: accumulate, as by natural growth. *When individuals are restrained from confronting life, they accrue a vast ability to have difficulties with it.*

additives: things which have been added. This usually has a bad meaning in that an *additive* is said to be something needless or harmful

439

which has been added to someone or something. For example, if a person was attacked or injured when he was young, he might still in present time be afraid of the type of situation or person that injured him, even if the present situation didn't call for such a reaction. This irrational fear is an additive. In common English, *additive* might mean a substance put into a compound to improve its qualities or suppress undesirable qualities. In Dianetics and Scientology it definitely means to add something resulting in undesirable results. *An individual becomes aberrated by additives.*

admin: a contraction or shortening of the word *administration*. It is used as a noun to denote the actions involved in administering an organization. The clerical and executive decisions, actions and duties necessary to the running of an organization, such as originating and answering mail, typing, filing, despatching, applying policy and all those actions, large and small, which make up an organization. *Admin* refers to the organizational functions of a job, as opposed to its technical aspects. [Bibliography: *Good Versus Bad Management, Admin Know-How Series 6, HCO PL 10 Nov. 66*]

affinity: degree of liking or affection or lack of it. Affinity is a tolerance of distance. A great affinity would be a tolerance of or liking of close proximity. A lack of affinity would be an intolerance of or dislike of close proximity. Affinity is one of the components of understanding. Further, and more germane to ability, if one could occupy the position of any part of life, one would feel a sufficient affinity for life to be able to merge with it or separate from it at will.

aggregate: gathered into or considered as a whole; total. *You could define* government as "that body created by the aggregate irresponsibility of a people."

alluding: referring in a casual or indirect way (to). "My child," is often the parent's fond manner of alluding to his offspring.

analytical mind: the conscious, aware mind which thinks, observes data, remembers it and resolves problems. It would be essentially the conscious mind as opposed to the unconscious mind. In Dianetics and Scientology the analytical mind is the one which is alert and aware and the reactive mind simply reacts without analysis. *See also* **reactive mind** *in this glossary. The individual is not his analytical mind, he is not his reactive mind, he is not his body any more than he is his house or his car.*

anatomy: what something is made up of or how it is put together. *It is an interesting commentary upon the mental anatomy of man that he seldom intends to do something good without actually accomplishing something good.*

antidote: something that prevents or counteracts injurious or unwanted effects. *Probably the problem is the antidote to unconsciousness.*

antipathetic: opposed or antagonistic in character, tendency, etc. *Evil is that item or activity antipathetic to the survival of oneself and his fellows.*

antiself: against self; hostile to self. *It is not realized generally that the criminal is not only antisocial but is antiself.*

arbitraries: things which are introduced into a situation without regard to the data of the situation. *[Reference: Organization Executive Course: "Orders Versus Arbitraries"]*

ARC: *a word made from the initial letters of Affinity, Reality and Communication which together equate to understanding. These are the three things necessary to the understanding of something—one has to have some affinity for it, it has to be real to him to some degree and he needs some communication with it before he can understand it. For more information on ARC, read the book The Problems of Work by L. Ron Hubbard. See also* **affinity**, **reality** *and* **communication** *in this glossary. [Reference: Lecture: "Gradients and ARC"]*

arduous: *marked by great labor or effort. When you find an individual who is bent entirely upon a course of the arduous control of the motions of others, you are looking at an individual who is afraid.*

armor plate: *a protective covering of steel plates, as on a tank. No sixteen-inch armor plate could possibly stop an idea.*

atomic fission: *the splitting of the nucleus of an atom into nuclei of lighter atoms, accompanied by the release of energy. This is the principle of the atomic bomb. There is no argument on Earth of sufficient emergency or violence to require war, much less war by atomic fission with the consequence of the destruction of at least one continent and, within a few years, the destruction of the planet Earth.*

auditing: *another word for processing, the application of Dianetics or Scientology processes to someone by a trained auditor. See also* **processing** *in this glossary. [Definition of preclear] Clear is the name of a* state achieved through auditing or an individual who has achieved this state.

auditor: a person trained and qualified in applying Dianetics and/or Scientology processes and procedures to individuals for their betterment; called an auditor because *auditor* means *one who listens*. See also **process** in this glossary. [Definition of *PAB*] *Their intent was to give the professional auditor and his preclears the best possible processes and processing available at the moment it became available.*

axiom: a statement of natural law on the order of those of the physical sciences. Full lists of the Axioms of Dianetics and the Axioms of Scientology are contained in the book *Scientology 0-8: The Book of Basics.* [Reference: **Technical Bulletin:** *"Axiom 28 Amended"*]

Bacon: Francis Bacon (1561–1626), English philosopher and author. He developed a method of thought in which he insisted that investigation must begin with observable facts. *Check your history and you will discover that the men whose marble busts adorn the modern halls of learning did not themselves have a formal education: Bacon, Spencer, Voltaire, etc., etc., etc., down the whole list; two or three exceptions prove the rule.*

balderdash: senseless talk or writing; nonsense. *It is actually pure balderdash and a sort of a weak limping apology for not being successful to say that one works for his own self-satisfaction.*

balked: blocked by an obstacle; hindered. *When it turns and faces the* *incomprehensible it feels balked and baffled, feels there is a secret, and feels that the secret is a threat to existence.*

barbarism: a barbarous (uncultured, uncivilized, unpolished) social or intellectual condition; absence of culture; uncivilized ignorance and rudeness. *Barbarism is the proper opposite of civilization. A nation may have huge machines, projectiles of great violence and stoves that do all the cooking and yet be a complete barbarism socially.*

bash: (colloquial) strike with a violent blow; smash. *Communication is the root of marital success from which a strong union can grow, and noncommunication is the rock on which the ship will bash out her keel.*

becomingness: the state, quality or an instance of becoming. *There is beingness, but man believes there is only becomingness.*

beingness: (1) condition or state of being; existence. *The fewer viewpoints which an individual will tolerate, the greater his occlusion and the worse his general state of beingness is.* (2) the assumption or choosing of a category of identity. *Beingness is assumed by oneself or given to oneself or is attained. Examples of beingness would be one's own name, one's profession, one's physical characteristics, one's role in a game—each and all of these things could be called one's beingness. It is even more important to be able to permit other people to have beingness than to be able oneself to assume it.*

benefactor: one who gives financial or other aid. *It is a rather noble commentary on man that when a person finds himself, as he believes, incapable of restraining himself from injuring a benefactor he will defend the benefactor by leaving.*

blaster: a weapon that emits a destructive blast. *It happens that a song is far more powerful than any blaster ever invented.*

blow-offs: a colloquialism (informal expression) for sudden departures. It is usually used to describe someone leaving or ceasing to be where he should really be. *[Reference: Technical Bulletin: "Blow-Offs"]*

bought: *(slang)* accepted as true, valid, agreeable, etc. *You can blame your whole confusion on the fact you bought illusion.*

brass: *(informal)* any very important officials. *No group can sit back and expect its high brass to be the only ones to carry the load.*

capital: any form of wealth employed or capable of being employed in the production of more wealth. *The only capital an executive has is the willingness to work.*

case: a person's condition; the way a person responds to the world around him by reason of his aberrations. *See also* **aberration** in this glossary. *If your mest is in disorder, your case is on the border.*

Chaplain: a staff post in a Scientology organization with the purpose of ministering to others, giving succor (aid, help, relief) to those who have been wronged and comforting those whose burdens have been too great. When preclears and students cannot elsewhere be heard, they always have recourse to the Chaplain. *See also* **preclear** in this glossary. *[Reference: Organization Executive Course: "Chaplain's Court, Civil Hearings"]*

Chaplain's Court: a hearing to resolve matters of dispute between individuals. A Chaplain's Court handles matters which are not ethics matters, but civil matters. *See also* **Chaplain** and **ethics** in this glossary. *[Reference: Organization Executive Course: "Chaplain's Court, Civil Hearings"]*

charlady: a woman who does cleaning or scrubbing, as in office buildings. *A charlady's concept of her own importance is far greater than that of a successful general manager!*

close-knit: tightly united, connected or organized. *They are not just the fodder of a close-knit group of initiates.*

cog: literally, a gear tooth; figuratively, a person who plays a minor part in a large organization, activity, etc. *They are not cogs in a mighty machine.*

communication: the interchange of ideas across space. Its full definition is the consideration and action of impelling an impulse or particle from source-point across a distance to receipt-point, with the intention of bringing into being at the receipt-point a duplication and understanding of that which emanated from the source-point. The formula of communication is cause, distance, effect, with intention, attention and duplication with understanding. *These component parts are affinity, reality and communication.*

communication lines: routes along which communication travels from one person to another; any sequences through which a message of any character may go. *He who holds the power of an organization is that person who holds its communication lines and who is a crossroad of the communications.*

conditions: the states of operation or existence which an individual, a group or an organization passes through. There are formulas connected with these operating states which, if handled properly, bring about stability, expansion, influence and well-being. For more information on conditions and their formulas, read *Introduction to Scientology Ethics* by L. Ron Hubbard. *[Reference: **Management Series:** "Conditions, How to Assign"]*

congress: an assembly of Scientologists held in any of various cities around the world for a presentation of Dianetics and/or Scientology materials. Many congresses were addressed directly by Ron. Others were based upon taped LRH lectures or films on a particular subject. *[Reference: **Freedom Congress Lectures**]*

covert: concealed; secret; disguised. *Insanity is the overt or covert but always complex and continuous determination to harm or destroy.*

crumb: *(slang)* a worthless or disgusting person. *The only thing that you ever object to in important people is that they act so thoroughly, too many times, on the supposition that everybody else is a crumb.*

curtailed: cut short; reduced. *Where an individual falls away from these his freedom is sharply curtailed and he finds himself confronted with barriers of magnitude.*

cynical: believing that people are motivated in all their actions only by selfishness; denying the sincerity of people's motives and actions or the value of living. *The critic but follows the fad of a cynical and apathetic age.*

demise: ceasing to exist; death. *It could be said that life was made to be lived, not died out of; and that facts which encourage a high level of living would be, for man, the most truthful facts; and that those which encourage his demise would be the most untruthful facts.*

Dianetics: Dianetics spiritual healing technology. It addresses and handles the effects of the spirit on the body and can alleviate such things as unwanted sensations and emotions, accidents, injuries and psychosomatic illnesses (ones that are caused or aggravated by mental stress). *Dianetics means "through the soul" (from Greek dia, through, and nous, soul). It is further defined as "what the soul is doing to the body." [Reference: Dianetics 55!]*

differentiation: the ability to "tell the difference" between one person and another, one object and another. It indicates a person is sane. As soon as one begins to confuse one's wife with one's mother, or one's coat with one's father's coat, one is on the road to insanity. *See also* **identification** *in this glossary. The greatest ability of thought is differentiation.*

disparage: speak slightingly of; say (something) is of less value or importance than it actually is; belittle. *Never disparage yourself or minimize your strength or power.*

dispensable: capable of being dispensed with or done without; not necessary or essential. *Men are not dispensable.*

doingness: the action of creating an effect. By *doing* is meant action, function, accomplishment, the attainment of goals, the fulfilling of purpose or any change of position in space. *The game of life demands that one assume a beingness in order to accomplish a doingness in the direction of havingness.*

dole: distribution by the government of relief payments to the unemployed. *When the organization is gone, there is only misery, the dole, revolution and sudden death.*

dowager: a widow with a title or property derived from her dead husband. *The rich man's son, the moneyed dowager, neither of them works.*

dramatizing: acting out; demonstrating. *A person who is dramatizing his criminal intent can become very angry if he is not prevented from hurting others.*

dynamic: of or relating to the motivating or driving force, physical or moral, in any field. *The dynamic principle of existence is survival.*

effect: the receipt point of a flow (thought, energy or action). For example: If one considers a river flowing to the sea, the place where it began would be the source-point or cause, and the place where it went into the sea would be the effect-point, and the sea would be the effect of the river. A man firing a gun is cause; a man receiving a bullet is effect. *See also* **source-point** *in this glossary. A fellow is a fool if he thinks that he can cause something without becoming one way or the other the effect of it.*

en masse: (French) in a mass; all together; as a group. *If you look at or listen to any work of art, there is only one thing the casual audience*

449

responds to en masse, and if this has it then you too will see it as a work of art.

ethics: rationality toward the highest level of survival for the individual, the future race, the group and mankind. Ethics is reason and the contemplation of optimum survival. A system of ethics exists in Scientology whereby a person can take certain actions to correct some conduct or situation in which he is involved which is contrary to the ideals and best interests of his group. Ethics consists simply of the actions an individual takes on himself. It is a personal thing. When one is ethical or "has his ethics in," it is by his own choice and is done by himself. [*Reference:* **Introduction to Scientology Ethics**]

evaluation: the imposing of data or knowledge upon another. An example would be to tell another why he is the way he is instead of permitting or guiding him to discover it for himself. People at low levels of awareness do not observe, but substitute for observation preconceptions, evaluation and suppositions, and even physical pain by which to attain their certainties.

fetter: confine; restrain. *"Competition" is a trick of the weak to fetter the strong.*

fixation: a concentration on one idea; an obsession. *Man's mortality, his "one life" fixation, all stem from his efforts to check himself, obliterate his memory in a fruitless effort to change his conduct and his self-destructive habits and impulses and losses of skills and abilities.*

flow: a progress of energy between two points. *Good management carefully* isolates all stops on its flow lines and eradicates them to increase speed of flows.

fodder: food in general. Used figuratively. *They are not just the fodder of a close-knit group of initiates.*

folly: a lack of sense or sensible conduct; foolishness. *When we look for neurosis and folly in our society we look toward those who do not or cannot work.*

forthright: *(figurative)* going straight to the point; straightforward; unswerving; outspoken. *All the effort in the world cannot overcome the idea of one forthright man, but a very small amount of thought can make a slave over a tremendous quantity of emotion and effort.*

germane: closely or significantly related; relevant; pertinent. *Further, and more germane to ability, if one could occupy the position of any part of life, one would feel a sufficient affinity for life to be able to merge with it or separate from it at will.*

gradients: the steps in a gradual approach to something taken step by step, level by level, each step or level being, of itself, easily attainable—so that finally, quite complicated and difficult activities can be achieved with relative ease. *[Reference: **Lecture:** "Gradients and ARC"]*

grant beingness: be able or willing to let someone else be what he is. Listening to what someone has to say and taking care to understand them, being courteous, refraining from needless criticism, expressing admiration or affinity are examples of the actions of someone who can grant others beingness. *See also **beingness** in this glossary. The ability* *to assume or to grant beingness is probably the highest of human virtues.*

hat: slang for the title and work of a post in a Scientology organization; taken from the fact that in many professions, such as railroading, the type of hat worn is the badge of the job. The term *hat* is also used to describe the write-ups, checksheets and packs that outline the purposes, know-how and duties of a post. It exists in folders and packs and is trained in on the person on the post. To *hat* someone is to train him on the functions and specialties of his post, and when a person is fully trained to do these he is said to be *hatted.* *[Reference: Organization Executive Course: "Model Hat for an Executive"]*

havingness: the concept of being able to reach. By havingness we mean owning, possessing, being capable of commanding, taking charge of objects, energies and spaces. The game of life demands that one assume a beingness in order to accomplish a doingness in the direction of havingness.

HCO: abbreviation for Hubbard Communications Office: the division of a Scientology organization which is responsible for the hiring of personnel, routing of incoming and outgoing communications and maintaining ethics and justice among Scientologists on staff and in the area. *See also* **ethics** in this glossary. *[Definition of HCOB]* abbreviation for Hubbard Communications Office Bulletin: a technical issue written by L. Ron Hubbard only.

HCOB: abbreviation for Hubbard Communications Office Bulletin: a technical issue written by L. Ron Hubbard only. An HCOB is valid from first issue unless specifically cancelled. All data for auditing and courses is contained in HCOBs. These outline the product of the organization. They are issued in red ink on white paper, consecutive by date. *See also* **auditing** *and* **HCO** *in this glossary.* *[Bibliography: Blow-Offs, HCOB 31 Dec. 59R]*

HCO PL: abbreviation for *Hubbard Communications Office Policy Letter:* a permanently valid issue of organization and administrative technology. HCO PLs, regardless of date or age, form the know-how of running an organization or group or company. These make up the bulk of staff hat materials in Scientology organizations. HCO PLs are signed by L. Ron Hubbard and issued in green ink on white paper, consecutive by date. *See also* **hat** *and* **HCO** *in this glossary.* *[Bibliography: Outflow, HCO PL 6 July 59 II]*

hell: any place or state of torment or misery. *To protect dishonest people is to condemn them to their own hells.*

hyacinth: a plant of the lily family, widely cultivated for its cylindrical cluster of fragrant flowers in a variety of colors. *He who said that a man who had two loaves of bread should sell one to buy white hyacinth, spoke sooth.*

identification: the inability to evaluate differences in time, location, form, composition or importance. *See also* **differentiation** *in this glossary.* *So long as one can differentiate, one is sane. Its opposite is identification.*

implicit: contained in the nature of something although not readily apparent. *It may be implicit or implied, emotional, conceptual or literal, inferred or stated.*

inflow: cause (something) to proceed inward toward oneself; receive. *He who would outflow must inflow—he who would inflow must outflow.*

initiates: those admitted into some society, office or position; those instructed in some secret knowledge. *They are not just the fodder of a close-knit group of initiates.*

invalidated: refuted, degraded, discredited or denied. *When we grow timid in the face of circumstance it is because our purpose, our stable data, have been invalidated.*

jingles: verses or tunes that have obvious, easy rhythm, simple rhymes, etc. *The "Dianetics Jingles" have been published as an appendix to The Route to Infinity lecture series transcripts. [Reference: The Route to Infinity Lectures: Appendix, "Dianetics Jingles"]*

keel: literally, the chief timber or steel piece along the entire length of the bottom of a ship or boat; figuratively, anything like a ship's keel in position, appearance, etc. *Communication is the root of marital success from which a strong union can grow, and noncommunication is the rock on which the ship will bash out her keel.*

knowingness: awareness not depending upon perception. One doesn't have to look to find out. For example, you do not have to get a perception or picture of where you are living to know where you live. *The basic difference between aberration and sanity, between inability* and ability, between illness and health, is the knowingness of causation by self opposed to unknown causation by others or other things.

liabilities: things that work against one; disadvantages. *So eager is a thetan to have a game that he will adopt to himself all manner of liabilities in order to have a parity with his opponents.*

lint: minute shreds or ravelings of yarn; bits of thread. *Actually, you are a giant tied down with cotton lint.*

livingness: the activity of going along a certain course, impelled (driven) by a purpose and with some place to arrive. *To have difficulties in life, all it is necessary to do is to start running away from the business of livingness.*

magnitude: great size, extent, importance or influence. *Where an individual falls away from these his freedom is sharply curtailed and he finds himself confronted with barriers of magnitude.*

manifests: makes clear or evident to the eye or the understanding; shows plainly. *Affinity manifests itself as the recognition of similarity of efforts and goals amongst organisms by those organisms.*

maw: anything thought of as consuming, devouring, etc., without end. *The creative, the constructive, the beautiful, the harmonious, the adventurous, yes, and even escape from the maw of oblivion: these things are pleasure and these things are necessity.*

mest: the physical universe. A word coined from the initial letters of Matter, Energy, Space and Time, which are the component parts (elements) of the physical universe. Also used loosely to mean physical universe objects, such as property or possessions. *If your mest is in disorder, your case is on the border.*

minions: servants or followers willing to do whatever they are ordered to do by their masters; henchmen. *And the man who has his ideals, no matter how thoroughly the minions of the devil may wheedle him to desert them, survives well only so long as he is true to those ideals.*

monitor: oversee, supervise or regulate. *Your ideas about yourself really don't monitor your behavior at all.*

mores: the customs, or customary practices, rules, etc., regarded as essential to or characteristic of a group. *What has made all man a pauper in his happiness? Transgressions against the mores of his race, his group, his family!*

morrow: the day following some specified day. *If you act in today you keep morrow away.*

neurosis: a condition wherein a person is insane or disturbed on some subject (as opposed to psychosis, wherein a person is just insane in general). *The common denominator of psychosis and neurosis is the inability to work.*

oblivion: the state of being completely forgotten or unknown. *The creative, the constructive, the beautiful, the harmonious, the adventurous, yes, and even escape from the maw of oblivion: these things are pleasure and these things are necessity.*

omnipresence: the fact of being present everywhere. *Entirely minus-freedom would be the omnipresence of barriers.*

organisms: living beings; individual animals or plants. *Affinity manifests itself as the recognition of similarity of efforts and goals amongst organisms by those organisms.*

outflow: cause (something) to issue or proceed outward from a source. *He who would outflow must inflow—he who would inflow must outflow.*

overt: open to view or knowledge; not concealed or secret. *Insanity is the overt or covert but always complex and continuous determination to harm or destroy.*

PAB: abbreviation for *Professional Auditor's Bulletin:* one of a series of issues written by L. Ron Hubbard between 10 May 1953 and 15 May 1959. The content of these bulletins is technical and promotional. Their intent was to give the professional auditor and his preclears the best possible processes and processing available at the moment it became available. *See also* **auditor, process** and **processing** in this glossary. *[Bibliography: The Anatomy of Failure, PAB 91, 3 July 56]*

paradox: a self-contradictory and false proposition. *"Art for art's sake" is a complete paradox as a remark.*

parity: equality, as in amount, status, character. *So eager is a thetan to have a game that he will adopt to himself all manner of liabilities in order to have a parity with his opponents.*

party: a person or group that participates in some action, affair, plan, etc.; participant. *While it is commonly believed to take two to make a fight, a third party must exist and must develop it for actual conflict to occur.*

post: a position, job or duty to which a person is assigned or appointed; an assigned area of responsibility and action in an organization which is supervised in part by an executive. *[Reference: Organization Executive Course: "Post, Handling Of"]*

postulate: a decision that something will happen. They are the victims of their own postulates, the victims of their own belief that they are inadequate.

preclear: a spiritual being who is now on the road to becoming Clear, hence pre-Clear. Clear is the name of a state achieved through auditing or an individual who has achieved this state. A Clear is an unaberrated person and is rational in that he forms the best possible solutions he can on the data he has and from his viewpoint. *See also* **auditing** in this glossary. *[Reference: Handbook for Preclears]*

preconceptions: ideas or opinions formed beforehand; biases or prejudices. People at low levels of awareness do not observe, but substitute for observation preconceptions, evaluation and suppositions, and even physical pain by which to attain their certainties.

present time: the time which is now, rather than in the past. It is a term loosely applied to the environment existing in the present. A person said to be "out of present time" would be someone whose attention is fixed on past events to such an extent that he is not fully aware of or in communication with his actual present environment. The avoidance of reality is merely an avoidance of present time.

process: a set of questions asked or commands given by a Scientology or

Dianetics practitioner to help a person find out things about himself or life and to improve his condition. *[Definition of **processing**] the application of Dianetics and/or Scientology processes and procedures to individuals for their betterment.*

processing: the application of Dianetics and/or Scientology processes and procedures to individuals for their betterment. The exact definition of processing is: The action of asking a person a question (which he can understand and answer), getting an answer to that question and acknowledging him for that answer. Also called *auditing*. See also **process** in this glossary. *[Reference: Mest Processing]*

projectiles: objects made to be shot with force through the air, such as cannon shells, bullets or rockets. *A nation may have huge machines, projectiles of great violence and stoves that do all the cooking and yet be a complete barbarism socially.*

psychosis: any severe form of mental disorder; insanity. *The common denominator of psychosis and neurosis is the inability to work.*

purchase: a hold or position of advantage for accomplishing something. *If you have no purpose, you have no purchase on the small, first particle necessary to make the whole understandable.*

racket: ramble or travel in a casual, reckless way, as in search of excitement. Used figuratively. *A song can racket down the ages.*

randomness: condition of being without definite aim, purpose or method, or adherence to a prior arrangement; existing in a haphazard way. *A confusion could be called an uncontrolled randomness.*

reactive: irrational, reacting instead of acting. *Man is not a reactive animal.*

reactive mind: that portion of a person's mind which works on a totally stimulus-response basis, which is not under his volitional control and which exerts force and the power of command over his awareness, purposes, thoughts, body and actions. *The individual is not his analytical mind, he is not his reactive mind, he is not his body any more than he is his house or his car.*

reality: the solid objects, the real things of life; the degree of agreement reached by two people. *These component parts are affinity, reality and communication.*

receipt-point: that which receives a communication; effect. *Communication is the consideration and action of impelling an impulse or particle from source-point across a distance to receipt-point, with the intention of bringing into being at the receipt-point a duplication and understanding of that which emanated from the source-point.*

remunerative: rewarding; profitable; well paid. *Outflow is holier, more moral, more remunerative and more effective than inflow.*

residual: remaining; still left. *Artistry, personal force, personality, all are residual in the basic personality.*

Scientology: Scientology philosophy. It is the study and handling of the spirit in relationship to itself, universes and other life. Scientology means *scio,* knowing in the fullest sense of the word and *logos,* study. In itself the word means literally *knowing how to know.* Scientology is a "route," a way, rather than a dissertation or an assertive body of knowledge. Through its drills and studies one may find the truth for himself. The technology is therefore not expounded as something to believe, but something to do. [Reference: *Scientology 8-8008*]

self-determined: exercising *self-determinism:* a condition of determining the actions of self; the ability to direct oneself. *The field of the arts must be of all things the most self-determined of any of man's activities.*

solvent: something that solves or explains. *Understanding is the universal solvent.*

sooth: truth. *He who said that a man who had two loaves of bread should sell one to buy white hyacinth, spoke sooth.*

soul food: (figurative) spiritual nourishment. *They are the soul food of all people.*

source-point: that from which something comes or develops; place of origin; cause. *Communication is the consideration and action of impelling an impulse or particle from source-point across a distance to receipt-point, with the intention of bringing into being at the receipt-point a duplication and understanding of that which emanated from the source-point.*

Spencer: Herbert Spencer (1820–1903), English philosopher. One of the few modern thinkers to attempt a systematic account of all cosmic (of the universe) phenomena, including mental and social principles. *Check your history and you will discover that the men whose marble busts adorn the modern halls of learning did not themselves have a formal*

461

education: Bacon, Spencer, Voltaire, etc., etc., etc., down the whole list; two or three exceptions prove the rule.

spike: something that stops one or spoils his chance for success. From the expression *spike (someone's) gun,* meaning to stop another from reaching a goal; to spoil someone's chance for success; to deny another pleasure; to punish. The expression *spike (someone's) gun* comes from the sabotaging technique of driving a spike into the vent of a gun barrel (the small hole at the back end of the barrel of a gun through which the charge is ignited), to prevent firing of the piece. *The only reason some people find ambition is a spike is they don't try to be, they try to be like.*

splurge: indulge oneself in some luxury or pleasure. *The greatest joy there is in life is creating. Splurge on it!*

studiously: zealously; wholeheartedly; deliberately. *The person who studiously avoids work usually works far longer and far harder than the man who pleasantly confronts it and does it.*

succumb: give way (to); yield; submit. *A primary trap is to succumb to invitations to hate.*

supposition: something supposed; assumption. *The only thing that you ever object to in important people is that they act so thoroughly, too many times, on the supposition that everybody else is a crumb.*

suppressive: acting to suppress, or squash, any betterment activity or group. *All a suppressive person or society is trying to do is prevent one from flourishing and prospering.*

teeth of, into the: directly and forcefully against. *And you make them into the teeth of old resolutions which were different.*

temper: state of mind; disposition; condition. *If you lump all the irresponsibility in a nation into one body you would then have an insane body. Thus the government temper.*

thetan: the person himself—not his body or his name, the physical universe, his mind, or anything else; that which is aware of being aware; the identity which is the individual. The term was coined to eliminate any possible confusion with older, invalid concepts. It comes from the Greek letter *theta* (θ), which the Greeks used to represent *thought* or perhaps *spirit*, to which an *n* is added to make a noun in the modern style used to create words in engineering. It is also θ^n, or "theta to the nth degree," meaning unlimited or vast. *The supreme test of a thetan is his ability to make things go right.*

thinkingness: that which has the capability of thinking and considering. *The soul is life, is the spirit, is the thinkingness, is the awareness or any such term which communicates to you the meaning of life and vitality.*

TR: abbreviation for training regimen or routine, often referred to as a training drill. TRs are practical drills which address (and can greatly increase) a student's ability in such areas as communication and control. See also **communication** in this glossary. *[Reference: The New Hubbard Professional TR Course]*

transgress: violate a law, command, moral code, etc.; offend; sin. *Share action with a group or person in your life, agree to mutually survive* by some specific code and then be cruel to them and so transgress and you'll have pain.

travail: pain, anguish or suffering resulting from mental or physical hardship. *Despite the amount of suffering, pain, misery, sorrow and travail which can exist in life, the reason for existence is the same reason as one has to play a game—interest, contest, activity and possession.*

truism: a self-evident, obvious truth. *It is a truism that if we could understand all life we would then tolerate all life.*

union: short for *labor union:* an organization of wage earners formed for the purpose of protecting the members' interests with respect to wages and working conditions. *A worker-oriented fellow—union leader, agitator, do-gooder—cares only for the worker and thus does the worker in.*

unthinkingness: the state, quality or an instance of lacking the ability to think; not being rational. *Unthinkingness has to do with a lack of ability to differentiate and a compulsion to identify unlike things with each other as though they were not only like things but the same thing.*

validation: the action of supporting or confirming the correctness, value or worth of someone or something. *Approval and validation are often far more valuable than material rewards and are usually worked for far harder than mere pay.*

valuable final products: (abbreviated *VFPs*) things that can be exchanged with other activities in return for support. The support usually adds up to food, clothing, shelter, money, tolerance and cooperation (goodwill). The actual precise definition of a VFP is that it must be valuable (can be exchanged elsewhere outside the area for something in return), final (does not need any further care or attention and is actually out of the shop totally) and product (something that was actually produced). A VFP is of course usually an object or a thing. It is something that can be counted. A thought or idea can become a VFP only if it emerges in concrete form in the physical universe and it can be exchanged only if you can carry it over and hand it to somebody and he can give you something back for it. *[Reference: Organization Executive Course: "Valuable Final Products"]*

viewpoint: a point from which to view. Any being is a viewpoint; he is as much a being as he is able to assume viewpoints. *In the opinion of the viewpoint, any beingness, any thing, is better than no thing, any effect is better than no effect, any universe better than no universe, any particle better than no particle, but the particle of admiration is best of all.*

Voltaire: assumed name of François Marie Arouet (1694–1778), French author and philosopher who believed in freedom of thought and respect for all men, and who spoke out against intolerance, tyranny and superstition. *Check your history and you will discover that the men whose marble busts adorn the modern halls of learning did not themselves have a formal education: Bacon, Spencer, Voltaire, etc., etc., etc., down the whole list; two or three exceptions prove the rule.*

welfare state: a state in which the welfare of the people in such matters as social security, health and education, housing and working conditions is the responsibility of the government. *The welfare state can be* defined as that state which rewards nonproduction at the expense of production.

wheedle: influence or persuade (a person) by flattery, soothing words, coaxing, etc. *And the man who has his ideals, no matter how thoroughly the minions of the devil may wheedle him to desert them, survives well only so long as he is true to those ideals.*

yap: (slang) noisy, stupid talk. *The whole yap of television and newspapers is directed toward reducing effort.*

yearns: has an earnest or strong desire; longs. *Fixed on too many barriers, man yearns to be free.*

zest: keen enjoyment; gusto. *Somehow the right to work seems to be bound up in happiness and the zest of living.*

Index

artist(s),

culture is only as great as its dreams, and its dreams are dreamed by, 158

stops his work when he believes he can no longer create an effect, 171

barrier(s),

defined, 212

fixed on too many barriers, man yearns to be free, 215

freedom among, 215

game consists of freedom, barriers and purposes, 228

man who is willing to accept restrictions and barriers, and is not afraid of them, is free, 218

beingness,

ability to assume or to grant beingness is probably the highest of human virtues, 71

game of life demands that one assume a beingness in order to accomplish a doingness in the direction of havingness, 239

there is beingness, but man believes there is only becomingness, 378

benefactor, when a person finds himself, as he believes, incapable of restraining himself from injuring a benefactor he will defend the benefactor by leaving, 391

blame,

being blamed sometimes blunts being cause, 189

blaming something else makes that something else cause, 184

if one's total ambition is to be blameless, the best situation is to get one's name on a tombstone, 189

body,

individual himself is a spirit controlling a body via a mind, 393

individual is not his body any more than he is his house or his car, 373

cause,

because some people cannot conceive of causing anything, they just watch it, 187

being blamed sometimes blunts being cause, 189

blaming something else makes that something else cause, 184

when life becomes serious, a man becomes less cause and greater effect, 188

you should not minimize yourself as cause, 176

certainty,

in creation, 303

is clarity of observation, 303

knowledge is a total certainty and understanding of data, 276

knowledge itself is certainty, 292

sanity is certainty, 306

to obtain a certainty one must be able to observe, 295

child(ren),

adult is the problem in child raising, 407

affection could no more spoil a child than the sun could be put out by a bucket of gasoline, 415

are not dogs, 405

basic difficulty with all juvenile delinquency, 413

best therapy a child can have, 409

forbidding children to work, 411

healthiest children come from the happiest mothers, 410

is a man or a woman who has not attained full growth, 407

spoiled child, 412

child(ren), *(cont.)*

when children become unimportant to a society, that society has forfeited its future, 404

you've lost the child forever that you seek to control and own, 412

civilization, is the sum total of its past and current contributors, 153

command, to command is to serve and only gives one the right to serve, 113

communicate,

he who can truly communicate to others is a higher being who builds new worlds, 29

if one gets himself into trouble by communicating, 31

man is as alive as he can communicate, 19

the most fundamental right of any being, 28

when in doubt, communicate, 21

communication(s),

component part of understanding, 10

defined, 18

do not give or receive communication unless you yourself desire it, 22

he who holds the power of an organization is that person who holds its communication lines, 101

is a two-way affair, 24

is the root of marital success, 26

more communication, not less, is the answer, 31

one could have conditions which appeared to be communications which were not, 23

unless one can originate communications one's imagination is in bad shape, 27

very unpopular in this society at this time to originate, 20

competence, 348

complexity, 280

degree of complexity is proportional to the degree of nonconfront, 258

conflict(s),

a third party must exist and must develop it for actual conflict to occur, 421

there are no conflicts which cannot be resolved unless the true promoters of them remain hidden, 420

confront,

basic thing man can't or won't confront is *evil*, 309

degree of simplicity is proportional to the degree of confront, 283

that which a person can confront, he can handle, 363

the less effort a being can confront, the more effect of effort he becomes, 347

to take apart a problem requires only to establish what one could not or would not confront, 256

confusion(s),

blame your whole confusion on the fact you bought illusion, 5

could be called an *uncontrolled randomness*, 323

defined, 298

is contagious, 318

is *random motion*, 298

is the basic cause of stupidity, 300

only a confusion so long as all particles are in motion, 299

those who cannot exert control actually breed confusions, 323

considerations, goodness and badness, beautifulness and ugliness are alike considerations and have no other basis than opinion, 265

contribute, human being feels able and competent
only so long as he is permitted to contribute
as much as or more than he has contributed
to him, 426

contribution,
rewards are not necessarily proportional to
contribution, 428
welfare state requiring no contribution will at
length be paid in revolution, 427

control,
anatomy of control is start, change and
stop, 324
defined, 322
good control and bad control, 333
individual who absolutely has to control
everything in sight is upsetting to all
of us, 329
just to have something to do and a reason to do
it exerts a control over life itself, 56
one's health and ability rise directly as one
asserts greater and surer control over his
surroundings, 335
people who are able to control something do not
need to be afraid of it, 327
secret of doing a good job is the secret of control
itself, 328

courage, there is a certain amount of courage
required in a leader, 100

coward, liar is inevitably a coward, the coward is
inevitably a liar, 197

crazy, the real crazy people in the universe, 178

creating, creation,
certainty in creation, 303
future is the creation of a future illusion, 57
greatest joy there is in life is creating, 79
highest purpose in the universe is the creation of
an effect, 49

creating, creation, (cont.)
those things which are scarce are those things
which the individual has lost his faith in
creating, 59

criminal(s),
accuses others of things which he himself is
doing, 196
are simply psychotic, 194
does not survive well, 43
is ignorant and stupid, 286
is in protest against his own survival, 200
is not only antisocial but is antiself, 200
nothing very glamorous about the, 194

criticism, attainment of one's standards is not
done by criticism, 334

culture,
individuals, and not masses, form the culture of
the race, 144
is only as great as its dreams, and its dreams
are dreamed by artists, 158

curse, no greater curse than total idleness, 82

data,
knowledge is not data, 292
stable datum is necessary to the alignment of
data, 301
thought does not necessarily have to be preceded
by data, but can create data, 289
when the data becomes a substitute for thinking
we have frozen the whole forward
progress of education, 278

dead,
how wrong can one be? Dead, 45
man is as dead as he can't communicate, 19
man who cannot work is as good as dead, 87
when a man is no longer able to envision
happiness as a part of his future, that
man is dead, 54

death,

    every impulse toward slavery is an impulse in the direction of misery, disease and death, 222

    failures are little bits of death, 230

    is a limited concept of the death of the physical part of the organism, 396

    man's ultimate in entrapment, 219

decision(s),

    child whose decisions have been interrupted continuously, 412

    is sanity and indecision is aberration, 314

    self-confidence is nothing more than belief in one's ability to decide and in one's decisions, 380

difficulties, to have difficulties in life, all it is necessary to do is to start running away from the business of livingness, 257

discipline, need for all discipline can be traced back to the inability to think, 285

doingness, game of life demands that one assume a beingness in order to accomplish a doingness in the direction of havingness, 239

doubt, when in doubt, communicate, 21

dream(s),

    are the stuff man uses for fuel, 53

    culture is only as great as its dreams, and its dreams are dreamed by artists, 158

    part of any dream is the man who dreamed it, 55

    without goals, hopes, ambitions or dreams, the attainment of pleasure is nearly impossible, 51

education,

    men whose marble busts adorn the modern halls of learning did not themselves have a formal education, 288–289

education, *(cont.)*

    when the data becomes a substitute for thinking we have frozen the whole forward progress of education, 278

effect,

    any effect is better than no effect, 374

    anything upon which you are not supposed to have any effect at all will sooner or later make you the unwilling or unknowing effect of it, 177

    art seeks to create an effect, 163

    artist stops his work when he believes he can no longer create an effect, 171

    fellow is a fool if he thinks that he can cause something without becoming one way or the other the effect of it, 183

    highest purpose in the universe is the creation of an effect, 49

    hope is simply a future possibility that one might have an effect on something, 180

    if one knows the tech of how to do something and can do it, and uses it, he *cannot* be the adverse effect of it, 357

    is not always created the *easy* way, 163

    when life becomes serious, a man becomes less cause and greater effect, 188

effort,

    all the effort in the world cannot overcome the idea of one forthright man, 61

    basic purpose of reason is the calculation or estimation of effort, 149

    less effort a being can confront, the more effect of effort he becomes, 347

    very small amount of thought can make a slave over a tremendous quantity of emotion and effort, 61

emergencies, are made—actively, 124

emotion,

people who cannot experience emotion because of their aberrations are ordinarily sick people, 399

without free emotion, an individual cannot appreciate as he should the pleasant things in his environment, 397

emotional, most people are not emotional—they are misemotional, 390

emotionalism, social order has confused irrationality with emotionalism, 296

entrapment,

is the opposite of freedom, 214

death itself could be said to be man's ultimate in entrapment, 219

the waiting one does for an answer, 24

environment,

every extinct species became extinct because it could not change to control a new environment, 340

man is as sane as he is dangerous to the environment, 341

man succeeds because he adjusts his environment to *him,* not by adjusting himself to the environment, 392

man thrives, oddly enough, only in the presence of a challenging environment, 35

when we say somebody should be in present time we mean he should be in communication with his environment, 13

evil,

basic thing man can't or won't confront is *evil,* 309

man is not trying to do evil, 310

only when he is beaten down below awareness as a chronic condition does man commit evil actions, 194

evil, *(cont.)*

that item or activity antipathetic to the survival of oneself and his fellows, 39

when man begins to do evil he seeks to destroy his memory in order to change and seeks to destroy his body, 198

executive(s),

common denominator to all good executives, 109

only capital an executive has is the *willingness to work,* 104

failure(s),

are little bits of death, 230

consists exactly of something else happening rather than the intention, 52

fear,

one does not have to enslave and control by force those whose conduct he does not fear, 330

that which one fears, one becomes, 361

unethical conduct is actually the conduct of destruction and fear, 197

fighting, most individuals are involved with fighting themselves, 377

flattery, is not very useful, 22

flourish(ing) and prosper(ing),

all a suppressive person or society is trying to do is prevent one from, 147

no more deadly way to get even with a suppressive or an antagonistic person or a downgrading society than by, 155

ultimate weapon is, 150

free,

if man cannot face what he is, then man cannot be free, 224

man who is willing to accept restrictions and barriers, and is not afraid of them, is free, 218

free, *(cont.)*

mind that is free is powerful, 220

no man who is not himself honest can
be free, 205

unhappy man is one who is considering
continually how to become free, 216

freedom,

all the power there is, is defined by and
contained in freedom, 220

among barriers, 215

depends on ability, 216

each and every impulse of freedom is an impulse
toward sanity, toward health, toward
happiness, 222

entrapment is the opposite of freedom, 214

for man does not mean freedom to injure
man, 209

is for honest people, 205

one impulse in man which cannot be erased is
his impulse toward freedom, 208

only possible way that you can get any freedom
is to stop asking everybody's permission
to be, 225

problem is more important than freedom, 244

the more matter, energy, time and space
assumes command over the individual the
less freedom that individual has, 212

friend,

healthy state of being is to be a friend to
yourself, 375

most neglected friend you have is you, 375

fun, an individual who can freely and with a clear
heart do things because they're fun is a very
sane person, 45

future,

imagination could be classified as the ability to
create or forecast a future, 60

future, *(cont.)*

is the creation of a future illusion and the working
toward that illusion to make it a reality, 57

sane person is concerned with the future, 317

game,

consists of freedom, barriers and purposes, 228

highest activity is playing a, 232

if anyone controlled everything he would
have no, 231

life has a motto that any game is better than
no game, 230

life is a, 228

of life demands that one assume a beingness in
order to accomplish a doingness in the
direction of havingness, 239

one loses every time one wins, for he then has
no game, 236

one never stops playing a game once
started, 234

reason for existence is the same reason as one
has to play a game—interest, contest,
activity and possession, 229

so eager is a thetan to have a game that he will
adopt to himself all manner of liabilities
in order to have a parity with his
opponents, 233

goal(s),

are the stuff man uses for fuel, 53

be true to your own goals, 63

is to win, 52

no man is happy without a goal, 53

part of a goal is its glamour, 55

thought is only as good as it can express the
goals and desires of man himself, 129

without goals, hopes, ambitions or dreams, the
attainment of pleasure is nearly
impossible, 51

government,
>if you lump all the irresponsibility in a nation into one body you would then have an insane body, 135
>"that body created by the aggregate irresponsibility of a people," 133

greatness,
>to love in spite of all is the secret of greatness, 70
>true greatness merely refuses to change in the face of bad actions against one, 425
>truly great person loves his fellows because he understands them, 425

group,
>individual initiative, not orders, makes a true group, 118
>is composed of individual group members, not of high brass, 118

happy, happiness,
>all the happiness you ever find lies in you, 66
>and strength endure only in the absence of hate, 70
>clue to happiness is being interested in life, 73
>could be said to be the overcoming of not unknowable obstacles toward a known and desirable goal, 73
>is a word which states a condition and the anatomy of that condition is interest, 79
>is power and power is being able to do what one is doing when one is doing it, 74
>men who cannot work are not happy men, 84
>no man is happy without a goal, 53
>one who is plotting how to get into things has a much better chance of becoming happy, 76
>people's happiness is as great as they can create it, 73

happy, happiness, *(cont.)*
>right to work seems to be bound up in happiness and the zest of living, 97
>there are no riches, gems or palaces as valued as mere happiness, 66
>to be happy, one only must be able to confront, which is to say, experience, those things that are, 75
>two rules for happy living, 68
>when a man is no longer able to envision happiness as a part of his future, that man is dead, 54

hate(d),
>a primary trap is to succumb to invitations to hate, 419
>happiness and strength endure only in the absence of hate, 70
>one is what one is, not what one is admired or hated for, 376

havingness, game of life demands that one assume a beingness in order to accomplish a doingness in the direction of havingness, 239

health,
>direct ratio between the health and ability of the person and his willingness to accept responsibility, 344
>each and every impulse of freedom is an impulse toward sanity, toward health, toward happiness, 222
>one's health and ability rise directly as one asserts greater and surer control over his surroundings, 335

help,
>one should help others to help themselves, 430
>when a person can no longer help he seeks to destroy, 311

honest(y),
freedom is for honest people, 205
individual rights were not originated to protect criminals but to bring freedom to honest men, 195
man who is known to be honest is awarded survival, 38
no man who is not himself honest can be free—he is his own trap, 205
right of a person to survive is directly related to his honesty, 193

hope, is simply a future possibility that one might have an effect on something, 180

idea(s),
all the effort in the world cannot overcome the idea of one forthright man, 61
and not battles mark the forward progress of mankind, 144
no sixteen-inch armor plate could possibly stop an, 145
wisdom is not a fixed, 284

idleness, no greater curse than total idleness, 82

ignorance,
and stupidity may therefore be called criminal, 286
only way a mind can be controlled is by enforcing upon it ignorance of itself, 326

illusion,
blame your whole confusion on the fact you bought illusion, 5
future is the creation of a future illusion and the working toward that illusion to make it a reality, 57

imagination,
could be classified as the ability to create or forecast a future or to create, change or destroy a present or past, 60

imagination, *(cont.)*
unless one can originate communications one's imagination is in bad shape, 27

immortal,
how right can one be? Immortal, 45
soul, 262, 393
thrust of survival is away from death and toward immortality, 34

important(ce),
asserting one's *own* importance is about as acceptable as a dead cat at a wedding, 112
nothing wrong with being the most important person under the sun, 72
only thing that you ever object to in important people, 112

indecision, decision is sanity and indecision is aberration, 314

individual(s),
himself is a spirit controlling a body via a mind, 393
is as live as he can consent to play the role he is playing, 240
is as well off as he can change things in location in space, 340
is not his analytical mind, he is not his reactive mind, he is not his body any more than he is his house or his car, 373
most individuals are involved with fighting themselves, 377
one never observes the *forced* individual doing a job well, 211
who can freely and with a clear heart do things because they're fun is a very sane person, 45

inflow,
he who would outflow must inflow—he who would inflow must outflow, 26

inflow, *(cont.)*

outflow is holier, more moral, more remunerative and more effective than inflow, 89

insane, insanity,

among the idle is a matter of problem scarcity, 250

are irresponsible, 314

denial of work is bound up with madness and insanity, 97

is contagious, 318

is the overt or covert but always complex and continuous determination to harm or destroy, 309

modern trend of "don't do" accompanies the modern trend of an increased percentage of the insane in the society, 313

road from insanity to sanity, 312

sane are constructive, the insane are destructive, 308

sane man has difficulty in insane surroundings, 319

sanity and insanity are matters of *motive*, not rationality or competence, 308

intelligence,

and judgment are measured by the ability to evaluate relative importances, 277

is the ability to perceive, pose and resolve problems, 250

interest(ed)(ing),

problems keep up interest, 244

clue to happiness is being interested in life, 73

thetan is interested, and an object is interesting, 185

when a person becomes terribly interesting he has lots of problems, 185

interest(ed)(ing), *(cont.)*

when one is no longer interested, but is only interesting, he has lost his principle quality as a thetan—freedom, and the ability to change at will, 186

invalidat(ed)(ion),

man has been invalidated to such an extent that he starts to do *himself* in—that's the secret of aberration, 401

self-invalidation is merely the accumulation of invalidation of oneself by others, 382

irresponsibility,

government, "that body created by the aggregate irresponsibility of a people," 133

if you lump all the irresponsibility in a nation into one body you would then have an insane body, 135

insane are irresponsible, 314

slavery is the consequence of irresponsibility and failure to do one's job, 90

joy, greatest joy there is in life is creating, 79

justice,

decent people are in favor of justice, 203

is one of the guards that keeps the channel of progress a channel and not a stopped flow, 123

only the criminally inclined are frightened enough of justice to protest and complain that it exists, 196

reasonably priced and easily obtained justice are requisites to any civilization, 153

knowledge,

body of knowledge cannot have an *opinion* on something, 270

insecurity exists in the absence of knowledge, 279

knowledge, *(cont.)*
> is a total certainty and understanding
> of data, 276
> itself is certainty; knowledge is *not* data, 292

leader,
> bad leadership isn't "grouchy"
> or "sadistic," 102
> certain amount of courage required in a
> leader, 100
> in all great leaders there is a purpose and
> intensity, 100
> man who merely wants to be liked will never be
> a leader, 100

liar,
> is inevitably a coward, the coward is inevitably
> a liar, 197
> no liar lying like an angry man, 268

lie(s),
> any problem, to be a problem, must contain
> a lie, 259
> are told because one is afraid of the
> consequences should one tell the
> truth, 197

life,
> energy is the byproduct of life, 184
> has a motto that any game is better than no
> game, 230
> in its highest state is understanding, 2
> is a game, 228
> is a group effort, 37
> itself does not die, 396
> poses problems for its own solution, 245
> was made to be lived, not died out of, 272

living,
> basic formula of *living* (not life) is *having and
> following a basic purpose,* 48

living, *(cont.)*
> itself is an art form, 167
> successes are little bits of living, 230
> two rules for happy living, 68

man('s)(men),
> all men are not created with equal potential
> value to their fellows, 345
> are not dispensable, 92
> greatest weapon is his reason, 149
> is an added-to being, 400
> is as alive as he can communicate, 19
> is basically good, 136, 198
> is capable of self-determinism, 388
> wherever man strives, wherever he works,
> whatever he does, the good he does
> outweighs the evil, 392

manager, good, 105

mankind,
> ideas and not battles mark the forward progress
> of mankind, 144
> lives and each man strives by codes of conduct
> mutually agreed, 192
> woman, arts and skills and creation and
> inspiration are her beauty, just as she is
> the beauty of mankind, 154

manners, are the lubrication that ease the
> frictions of social contacts, 419

mest, 331

mind,
> easiest thing a thetan does is change his mind,
> 339
> only way a mind can be controlled is by
> enforcing upon it ignorance of itself, 326
> snapping bright mind and an alert body are
> worth a hundred thousand years of
> "experience" behind some dusty desk or
> counter, 288

past, *(cont.)*

you are treating yourself in present time much as you were treated by others in the past, 371

peace, on the day when we can fully trust each other, there will be peace on Earth, 431

people,

are willing to do their best and will until hammered about it, 102

have value and are important, 69

ignore people at your peril, 110

you have no idea how important people are, 111

perfection, seeking perfection is a wrong target in art, 166

persist,

anything which is not directly observed tends to persist, 258

that which is not admired tends to persist, 424

personality, life and the personality, apparently, go on, 396

pleasure,

is not less valid in survival than the avoidance of pain, 43

there is a necessity for pleasure, 44

without goals, hopes, ambitions or dreams, the attainment of pleasure is nearly impossible, 51

politics, only difference in existing systems of politics is their relative values in giving the individual a chance to develop, 140

positiveness, 103

potentialities, your potentialities are a great deal better than anyone ever permitted you to believe, 346

power,

an individual is basically and routinely good, capable of many actions and considerable power, 398

happiness is power and power is being able to do what one is doing when one is doing it, 74

mind that is free is powerful, 220

never disparage yourself or minimize your strength or power, 384

of a thetan stems from his ability to hold a position in space, 384

one cannot hold power and not use it, 101

problem(s),

any problem, to be a problem, must contain a lie, 259

basic anatomy of that problem is purpose—counter-purpose, 246

consists of two or more purposes opposed, 246

insanity among the idle is a matter of problem scarcity, 250

is certainly the antidote for boredom, 253

is more important than freedom, 244

is the antidote to unconsciousness, 253

keep up interest, 244

life poses problems for its own solution, 245

man very often solves his problems from his own point of view only, 136

person lacks problems, opponents and counter-purposes to his own, *he will invent them,* 252

put a man in a position where he can solve his own problems, 249

thetan loves a problem, 251

to take apart a problem requires only to establish what one could not or would not confront, 256

right(s)(ness), *(cont.)*
    of a person to survive is directly related to his
        honesty, 193
    one tries to be right *always*, 180
    supreme test of a thetan is his ability to make
        things go right, 176
    the most fundamental right of any being is the
        right to communicate, 28
    to command is to serve and only gives one the
        right to serve, 113

role, individual is as live as he can consent to play
    the role he is playing, 240

sane,
    are constructive, the insane are destructive, 308
    man has difficulty in insane surroundings, 319
    man is as sane as he is dangerous to the
        environment, 341
    person is concerned with the future, 317

sanity,
    and insanity are matters of *motive*, not
        rationality or competence, 308
    decision is sanity and indecision is
        aberration, 314
    is certainty, 306
    is the ability to recognize differences, similarities
        and identities, 307
    road from insanity to sanity, 312
    road to sanity is demonstrably the road to
        increasing certainty, 319
    true sanity defined, 255
    true sign of sanity and greatness, 418
    you can't beat a man into sanity, 311

secret(s),
    greatest secret in this universe, 70
    is a threat to existence, 6
    the answer which was never given, 25

self-confidence,
    alone is security, 351
    is nothing more than belief in one's ability to
        decide and in one's decisions, 380

self-determinism, 388

self-satisfaction, 170

simple, all answers are basically simple, 282

simplicity, degree of simplicity is proportional to
    the degree of confront, 283

slavery,
    is the consequence of irresponsibility and failure
        to do one's job, 90
    man cannot afford slavery, 151

society,
    delete from a society its willingness to
        participate and its willingness to work,
        and you've killed the society, 128
    one never observes a *forced* society winning
        against an equally prosperous free
        society, 211
    to be denied the right to work is to be denied
        any part of the society in which we
        live, 85
    when children become unimportant to a society,
        that society has forfeited its future, 404

solvent, understanding is the universal solvent, 8

song, is far more powerful than any blaster ever
    invented, 159

space, power of a thetan stems from his ability to
    hold a position in space, 384

spectators, 187

speed,
    good management carefully isolates all stops on
        its flow lines and eradicates them to
        increase speed of flows, 108

speed, *(cont.)*

    prosperity of any organization is directly
        proportional to the speed of its
        particles, 120

spirit,

    ask somebody, "What is a spirit," and you
        might as well ask, "How are you?" 394
    individual himself is a spirit controlling a body
        via a mind, 393
    soul is life, is the spirit, is the thinkingness, is
        the awareness or any such term which
        communicates to you the meaning of life
        and vitality, 395

stable datum (data), 300

    is necessary to the alignment of data, 301
    when we grow timid in the face of circumstance
        it is because our purpose, our stable data,
        have been invalidated, 301

strong,

    "Competition" is a trick of the weak to fetter
        the strong, 237
    one is done wrong by the weaklings of this
        world, not by the strong men, 330

stupidity,

    confusion is the basic cause of stupidity, 300
    the criminal is ignorant and stupid; ignorance
        and stupidity may therefore be called
        criminal, 286

survival,

    a man who is known to be honest is awarded
        survival, 38
    man, in affinity with man, survives, and that
        survival is pleasure, 41
    pleasure is not less valid in survival than the
        avoidance of pain, 43
    rightness is conceived to be survival, 45

survival, *(cont.)*

    the criminal is in protest against his own
        survival, 200
    the dynamic principle of existence is
        survival, 34
    the goals of man, then, stem from the single
        goal of survival through a conquest of the
        material universe, 36
    the only real guarantee of survival is
        abundance, 40
    thrust of survival is away from death and
        toward immortality, 34

technical expertise, 165

teenagers, forbidding teenagers to make their own
    way in the world and earn their own
    money, 411

thetan,

    is interested, and an object is interesting, 185
    loves a problem, 251
    power of a thetan stems from his ability to hold
        a position in space, 384
    principle quality as a, 186
    supreme test of a, 176

third party, must exist and must develop it for
    actual conflict to occur, 421

thought,

    a very small amount of thought can make a
        slave over a tremendous quantity of
        emotion and effort, 61
    is only as good as it can express the goals and
        desires of man himself, 129

time, essence of time is change, 58

today,

    if you act in today you keep morrow away, 366
    life is in you today, and you make your
        tomorrow, 385

tomorrow,

life is in you today, and you make your tomorrow, 385

one inherits tomorrow what he died out of yesterday, 155

trap(s),

a primary trap is to succumb to invitations to hate, 419

endless desire for *freedom from* is a perfect trap, 213

individual only gets into traps and circumstances he intends to get into, 223

is always preceded by one's own choice of entrance, 223

no man who is not himself honest can be free—he is his own trap, 205

only trap into which life can fall is to do things without knowing it is doing them, 365

true,

all you can get anybody to do is inspect himself, his environment, life, and find out what's true for him, 273

what is true for you is what you have observed yourself, 266

trust, on the day when we can fully trust each other, there will be peace on Earth, 431

truth, 267

is actually a relative quantity, 263

is built by those who have the breadth and balance to see also where they're wrong, 268

is not determined by its appeal but by the evidence, 271

understand(ing),

component parts of, 10

if we could understand all life we would then tolerate all life, 9

understand(ing), *(cont.)*

is the universal solvent, 8

life in its highest state is, 2

no understanding, 3

only personal contact can restore, 15

the only richness there is, 4

unhappiness,

inability to confront that which is, 75

state of mind which insists only upon freedom can bring about nothing but, 77

unhappy,

man is one who is considering continually how to become free, 216

no more unhappy thing than a man who has accomplished all his ends in life, 62

universe,

any universe better than no universe, 374

one can't be totally safe in this universe, 85

victim(s),

one cannot go through life victimizing one's fellow beings and wind up in anything but a trap—the victim himself, 210

people are the victims of their own flinch, 360

viewpoint(s),

a thing to be "good" would depend on the viewpoint of the observer, and the same condition would exist for "bad," 264

the fewer viewpoints which an individual will tolerate, the greater his occlusion and the worse his general state of beingness is, 10

war,

criminality and war, 134

no argument on Earth of sufficient emergency or violence to require war, 148

no war ever earned anything but war, 150

way, the way out is the way through, 358

wealth, 129

win(s),

the goal is to win, 52

one loses every time one wins, for he then has no game, 236

wisdom,

I know no man who has any monopoly upon the wisdom of this universe, 273

is not a fixed idea, 284

one should share what wisdom he has, 430

wise man,

confronted with conflicting data, realizes that he knows at least one thing—that he doesn't know, 287

no wise man should stammer because another shuns his grammar, 28

tests before he talks, 284

withdraws, that which a person withdraws from in this universe becomes, to a marked degree, his master, 359

woman, arts and skills and creation and inspiration are her beauty, just as she is the beauty of mankind, 154

work,

children, in the main, are quite willing to work, 406

common denominator of psychosis and neurosis is the inability to work, 82

denial of work is bound up with madness and insanity, 97

forbidding children to work, 411

is only as good as it's enjoyed, not as it's paid, 129

work, *(cont.)*

man who cannot work is as good as dead, 87

men who cannot work are not happy men, 84

no good worker *owes* his work, 95

right to work seems to be bound up in happiness and the zest of living, 97

when a man is whipped, that work he then does still stems from his willingness alone, 104

when we look for neurosis and folly in our society we look toward those who do not or cannot work, 91

wrong,

all wrong actions are the result of an error followed by an insistence on having been right, 181

always last sung song, "I was wrong," 423

how wrong can one be? Dead, 45

truth is built by those who have the breadth and balance to see also where they're wrong, 268

yesterday, never regret yesterday, 385

you, yourself,

healthy state of being is to be a friend to yourself, 375

life is in you today, and you make your tomorrow, 385

most neglected friend you have is you, 375

never disparage yourself or minimize your strength or power, 384

Bibliography

The quotes in this book were taken from the books, lectures, issues and articles by L. Ron Hubbard listed below. More data on the books and many of the lectures can be found on the following pages. For copies of these materials, contact any of the addresses given in the list at the back of this book.

Books:

A New Slant on Life
Advanced Procedure and Axioms
Child Dianetics
Creation of Human Ability, The
Dianetics 55!
Dianetics: The Evolution of a Science
Dianetics: The Modern Science of Mental Health
Dynamics of Life, The
Handbook for Preclears
How to Live Though an Executive
Introduction to Scientology Ethics
Notes on the Lectures of L. Ron Hubbard
Problems of Work, The
Science of Survival

Scientology 0-8: The Book of Basics
Scientology 8-8008
Scientology: The Fundamentals of Thought
Self Analysis

Organization Executive Course Issues:

Management Series Issues:

Technical Bulletins:

Course Materials:

Hubbard Life Orientation Course, The
New Hubbard Professional TR Course, The

Personal Achievement Series Lectures:

Differences Between Scientology and Other Studies

Health and Certainty
Increasing Efficiency
Man: Good or Evil
Man's Relentless Search
Miracles
Scientology and Effective Knowledge
The Road to Perfection, The Goodness of Man

Lecture Series:

Freedom Congress Lectures
Philadelphia Doctorate Course Lectures, The
Phoenix Lectures, The
Route to Infinity Lectures, The

Other Lectures:

Attack on the Preclear, 6 Mar. 52
Cause and Effect: Education, Unknowing Effect, 30 Dec. 57
Control, 22 July 57
Gradients and ARC, 1 Sept. 66

Filmed Interview:

"An Introduction to Scientology"

Articles:

Books and Tapes
by L. Ron Hubbard

Basic Scientology Books

The *Basic Scientology Books Package* contains the knowledge you need to be able to improve conditions in life. These books are available individually or as a set, complete with an attractive slipcase.

Scientology: The Fundamentals of Thought • Improve life and make a better world with this easy-to-read book that lays out the fundamental truths about life and thought. No such knowledge has ever before existed, and no such results have ever before been attainable as those which can be reached by the use of this knowledge. Equipped with this book alone, one could perform seeming miracles in changing the states of health, ability and intelligence of people. This *is* how life works. This *is* how you change men, women and children for the better, and attain greater personal freedom.

A New Slant on Life. Have you ever asked yourself *Who am I? What am I?* This book of articles by L. Ron Hubbard answers these all-too-common questions. This is knowledge one can use every day— for a new, more confident and happier slant on life!

The Problems of Work. Work plays a big part in the game of life. Do you really enjoy your work? Are you certain of your job security? Would you like the increased personal satisfaction of doing your work well? This is the book that shows exactly how to achieve these things and more. The game of life—and within it, the game of work—can be enjoyable and rewarding.

Scientology 0-8: The Book of Basics. What is life? Did you know an individual can create space, energy and time? Here are the basics of life itself, and the secrets of becoming cause over any area of your life. Discover how you can use the data in this book to achieve your goals.

Basic Dictionary of Dianetics and Scientology. Compiled from the works of L. Ron Hubbard, this convenient dictionary contains the terms and expressions needed by anyone learning Dianetics and Scientology technology. And a *special bonus*—an easy-to-read Scientology organizing board chart that shows you who to contact for services and information at your nearest Scientology organization.

OT[1] Library Package

All the following books contain the knowledge of a spiritual being's relationship to this universe and how his abilities to operate successfully in it can be restored. You can get all of these books individually or in a set, complete with an attractive slipcase.

Scientology 8-80 • What are the laws of life? We are all familiar with physical laws such as the law of gravity, but what laws govern life and thought? L. Ron Hubbard answers the riddles of life and its goals in the physical universe.

Scientology 8-8008 • Get the basic truths about your nature as a spiritual being and your relationship to the physical universe around you. Here, L. Ron Hubbard describes procedures designed to increase your abilities to heights previously only dreamed of.

Scientology: A History of Man • A fascinating look at the evolutionary background and history of the human race—revolutionary concepts guaranteed to intrigue you and challenge many basic assumptions about man's true power, potential and abilities.

---

1. *OT*: abbreviation for **Operating Thetan**, a state of beingness. It is a being "at cause over matter, energy, space, time, form and life." *Operating* comes from "able to operate without dependency on things," and *Thetan* is the Greek letter *theta* (θ), which the Greeks used to represent *thought* or perhaps *spirit*, to which an *n* is added to make a noun in the modern style used to create words in engineering. It is also θ^n or "theta to the nth degree," meaning unlimited or vast.

The Creation of Human Ability. This book contains processes designed to restore the power of a thetan over his own postulates, to understand the nature of his beingness, to free his self-determinism and much, much more.

Basic Dianetics Books

The Basic Dianetics Books Package is your complete guide to the inner workings of the mind. You can get all of these books individually or in a set, complete with an attractive slipcase.

Dianetics: The Modern Science of Mental Health. Acclaimed as the most effective self-help book ever published. Dianetics technology has helped millions reach new heights of freedom and ability. Millions of copies are sold every year! Discover the source of mental barriers that prevent you from achieving your goals—and how to handle them!

The Dynamics of Life. Break through the barriers to your happiness. This is the first book Ron wrote detailing the startling principles behind Dianetics—facts so powerful they can change forever the way you look at yourself and your potentials. Discover how you can use the powerful basic principles in this book to blast through the barriers of your mind and gain full control over your success, future and happiness.

Self Analysis • The complete do-it-yourself handbook for anyone who wants to improve their abilities and success potential. Use the simple, easy-to-learn techniques in *Self Analysis* to build self-confidence and reduce stress.

Dianetics: The Evolution of a Science • It is estimated that we use less than ten percent of our mind's potential. What stops us from developing and using the full potential of our minds? *Dianetics: The Evolution of a Science* is L. Ron Hubbard's incredible story of how he discovered the reactive mind and how he developed the keys to unlock its secrets. Get this firsthand account of what the mind really is, and how you can release its hidden potential.

Dianetics Graduate Books

These books by L. Ron Hubbard give you detailed knowledge of how the mind works—data you can use to help yourself and others break out of the traps of life. While you can get these books individually, the Dianetics Graduate Books Package can also be purchased as a set, complete with an attractive slipcase.

Science of Survival • If you ever wondered why people act the way they do, you'll find this book a wealth of information. It's vital to anyone who wants to understand others and improve personal relationships. *Science of Survival* is built around a remarkable chart—the Hubbard Chart of Human Evaluation. With it you can understand and predict other people's behavior and reactions and greatly increase your control over your own life. This is a valuable handbook that can make a difference between success and failure on the job and in life.

Dianetics 55! • Your success in life depends on your ability to communicate. Do you know a formula exists for communication? Learn the rules of better communication that can help you live a more fulfilling life. Here, L. Ron Hubbard deals with the fundamental principles of communication and how you can master these to achieve your goals.

Advanced Procedure and Axioms • For the *first* time the basics of thought and the physical universe have been codified into a set of fundamental laws, signaling an entirely new way to view and approach the subjects of man, the physical universe and even life itself.

Handbook for Preclears • Written as an advanced personal workbook, *Handbook for Preclears* contains easily done processes to help you overcome the effect of times you were not in control of your life, times that your emotions were a barrier to your success and much more. Completing all the fifteen auditing steps contained in this book sets you up for really being in *control* of your environment and life.

Child Dianetics • Here is a revolutionary new approach to rearing children with Dianetics auditing techniques. Find out how you can help your child achieve greater confidence, more self-reliance, improved learning rate and a happier, more loving relationship with you.

Notes on the Lectures of L. Ron Hubbard • *Compiled from his fascinating lectures given shortly after the publication of* Dianetics, *this book contains some of the first material Ron ever released on the ARC triangle and the Tone Scale, and how these discoveries relate to auditing.*

Basic Executive Books

The Basic Executive Books Package consists of the book *The Problems of Work* and the two books listed below. They are available individually or as a set, complete with an attractive slipcase.

How to Live Though an Executive • *What are the factors in business and commerce which, if lacking, can keep a person overworked and worried, keep labor and management at each other's throats, and make an unsafe working atmosphere? L. Ron Hubbard reveals principles based on years of research into many different types of organizations.*

Introduction to Scientology Ethics • *A complete knowledge of ethics is vital to anyone's success in life. Without knowing and applying the information in this book, success is only a matter of luck or chance. That is not much to look forward to. This book contains the answers to questions like, "How do I know when a decision is right or wrong?" "How can I predictably improve things around me?" The powerful ethics technology of L. Ron Hubbard is your way to ever-increasing survival.*

Purification Book Package

The books in the Purification Book Package contain data on the only effective way of handling drug and toxic residuals in the body, clearing the way for real mental and spiritual improvement—the Purification program. These books are available individually and as a specially boxed set.

Clear Body, Clear Mind: The Effective Purification Program● This book contains all the information on L. Ron Hubbard's Purification program. This is the only program of its kind in existence that has been found to clean the residues of drugs, toxins and elements harmful to human bodies out of them! Drugs and chemicals can stop a person's ability to improve himself or just to live life. This book describes the program which can make it possible to start living again.

Purification: An Illustrated Answer to Drugs ● Presented in a concise, fully illustrated format, this book provides you with an overview of the Purification program. Our society is ridden by abuse of drugs, alcohol and medicine that reduce one's ability to think clearly. This book lays out what can be done about it, in a form which is easy for anyone to read and understand.

Purification Rundown Delivery Manual● This book is a manual which guides a person through the Purification Rundown step by step. It includes all of the needed reports as well as spaces for the person to write his successes and to attest to program completion. This manual makes administering the Purification Rundown simple and standard.

All About Radiation • Can the effects of radiation exposure be avoided or reduced? What exactly would happen in the event of an atomic explosion? Get the answers to these and many other questions in this illuminating book. *All About Radiation* describes observations and discoveries concerning the physical and mental effects of radiation and the possibilities for handling them. Get the real facts on the subject of radiation and its effects.

Other Scientology Books

Have You Lived Before This Life? • This is the book that sparked a flood of interest in the ancient puzzle: Does man live only one life? The answer lay in mystery, buried until L. Ron Hubbard's researches unearthed the truth. Actual case histories of people recalling past lives in auditing tell the tale.

Background and Ceremonies of the Church of Scientology • Discover the beautiful and inspiring ceremonies of the Church of Scientology, and its fascinating religious and historical background. This book contains the illuminating Creed of the Church, church services, sermons and ceremonies, many as originally given in person by L. Ron Hubbard, Founder of Scientology.

What Is Scientology? • Scientology applied religious philosophy has attracted great interest and attention since its beginning. What is Scientology philosophy? What can it accomplish—and why are so many people from all walks of life proclaiming its effectiveness? Find the answers to these questions and many others in *What Is Scientology?*

Dianetics and Scientology Technical Dictionary. • This dictionary is your indispensable guide to the words and ideas of Scientology and Dianetics technologies—technologies which can help you increase your know-how and effectiveness in life. Over three thousand words are defined—including a new understanding of vital words like *life, love* and *happiness* as well as Scientology terms.

Modern Management Technology Defined: Hubbard Dictionary of Administration and Management • Here's a real breakthrough in the subject of administration and management! Eighty-six hundred words are defined for greater understanding of any business situation. Clear, precise Scientology definitions describe many previously baffling phenomena and bring truth, sanity and understanding to the often murky field of business management.

Organization Executive Course • The *Organization Executive Course* volumes contain organizational technology never before known to man. This is not just how a Scientology organization works; this is how the operation of *any* organization, *any* activity, can be improved. A person knowing the data in these volumes fully, and applying it, could completely reverse any downtrend in a company—or even a country!

Management Series Volumes 1 and 2 • These books contain technology that anyone who works with management in any way must know completely to be a true success. Contained in these books are such subjects as data evaluation, the technology of how to organize any area for maximum production and expansion, how to handle personnel, the actual technology of public relations and much more.

Introductory and Demonstration Processes and Assists • How can you help someone increase his enthusiasm for living? How can you improve someone's self-confidence on the job? Here are basic Scientology processes you can use to help others deal with life and living.

Volunteer Minister's Handbook • This is a big, practical how-to-do-it book to give a person the basic knowledge on how to help self and others through the rough spots in life. It consists of twenty-one sections—each one covering important situations in life, such as drug and alcohol problems, study difficulties, broken marriages, accidents and illnesses, a failing business, difficult children, and much more. This is the basic tool you need to help someone out of troubles, and bring about a happier life.

Research and Discovery Series • These volumes contain the only existing day-to-day, week-to-week record of the progress of L. Ron Hubbard's research in Dianetics and Scientology. Through the pages of these beautiful volumes you follow L. Ron Hubbard's fantastic research adventure, beginning in the depths of man's degradation and obsession with the material universe and soaring to the realms of the spirit, freed from the bondage of the past.

Technical Bulletins • These volumes contain all of L. Ron Hubbard's technical bulletins and issues from the earliest to the latest. Almost any technical question can be answered from the pages of these volumes, which also include an extremely extensive master subject index.

The Personal Achievement Series

There are nearly three thousand recorded lectures by L. Ron Hubbard on the subjects of Dianetics and Scientology. What follows is a sampling of these lectures, each known and loved the world over. All of these are presented in Clearsound state-of-the-art sound-recording technology, notable for its clarity and brilliance of reproduction.

Get all the Personal Achievement Series cassettes by L. Ron Hubbard listed below and ask your nearest Scientology church or organization or the publisher about future releases.

The Story of Dianetics and Scientology • In this lecture,

L. Ron Hubbard shares with you his earliest insights into human nature and gives a compelling and often humorous account of his experiences. Spend an unforgettable time with Ron as he talks about the start of Dianetics and Scientology!

The Road to Truth. The road to truth has eluded man since the beginning of time. In this classic lecture, L. Ron Hubbard explains what this road actually is and why it is the only road one MUST travel all the way once begun. This lecture reveals the only road to higher levels of living.

Scientology and Effective Knowledge. Voyage to new horizons of awareness! *Scientology and Effective Knowledge* by L. Ron Hubbard can help you understand more about yourself and others. A fascinating tale of the beginnings of Dianetics and Scientology.

The Deterioration of Liberty. What do governments fear so much in a population that they amass weapons to defend themselves from people? Find out from Ron in this classic lecture.

Power of Choice and Self-Determinism. Man's ability to determine the course of his life depends on his ability to exercise his power of choice. Find how you can increase your power of choice and self-determinism in life from Ron in this lecture.

Scientology and Ability. Ron points out that this universe is here because we perceive it and agree to it. Applying Scientology principles to life can bring new adventure to life and put you on the road to discovering better beingness.

The Hope of Man. Various men in history brought forth the idea that there was hope of improvement. But L. Ron Hubbard's discoveries in Dianetics and Scientology have made that hope a reality. Find out by listening to this lecture how Scientology has become man's one, true hope for his final freedom.

The Dynamics. In this lecture Ron gives incredible data on the dynamics: how man creates on them, what happens when a person gets stuck in just one, how wars relate to the third dynamic and much more.

Money. Ron talks in this classic lecture about that subject which makes or breaks men with the greatest of ease—money. Find out what money really is and gain greater control over your own finances.

Formulas for Success—*The Five Conditions.* How does one achieve real success? It sometimes appears that luck is the primary factor, but the truth of the matter is that natural laws exist which govern the conditions of life. These laws have been discovered by Ron, and in this lecture he gives you the exact steps to take in order to improve conditions in any aspect of your life.

Health and Certainty. You need certainty of yourself in order to achieve the success you want in life. In *Health and Certainty,*

L. Ron Hubbard tells how you can achieve certainty and really be free to think for yourself. Get this tape now and start achieving your full potential!

Operation Manual for the Mind • Everybody has a mind— but who has an operation manual for it? This lecture reveals why man went on for thousands of years without understanding how his mind is supposed to work. The problem has been solved. Find out how with this tape.

Miracles • Why is it that man often loses to those forces he resists or opposes? Why can't an individual simply overcome obstacles in life and win? In the tape lecture *Miracles*, L. Ron Hubbard describes why one suffers losses in life. He also describes how a person can experience the miracles of happiness, self-fulfillment and winning at life. Get a copy today.

The Road to Perfection—*The Goodness of Man* • Unlike earlier practices that sought to "improve" man because he was "bad," Scientology assumes that you have good qualities that simply need to be increased. In *The Road to Perfection*, L. Ron Hubbard shows how workable this assumption really is—and how you can begin to use your mind, talents and abilities to the fullest. Get this lecture and increase your ability to handle life.

The Dynamic Principles of Existence • What does it take to survive in today's world? It's not something you learn much about in school. You have probably gotten a lot of advice about how to "get along." *Your survival right now is limited by the data you were given.* This lecture describes the dynamic principles of existence, and tells how you can use these principles to increase your success in all areas of life. Happiness and self-esteem can be yours. Don't settle for anything less.

Man: Good or Evil? • In this lecture, L. Ron Hubbard explores the greatest mystery that has confronted modern science and philosophy—the true nature of man's livingness and beingness. Is man simply a sort of wind-up doll or clock—or worse, an evil beast with no control of his cravings? Or is he capable of reaching higher levels of ability, awareness and happiness? Get this tape and find out the *real* answers.

Differences between Scientology and Other Studies • The most important questions in life are the ones you started asking as a child: What happens to a person when he dies? Is man basically good, or is he evil? What are the intentions of the world toward me? Did my mother and father really love me? What is love? Unlike other studies, which try to *force* you to think a certain way, Scientology enables you to find your own answers. Listen to this important lecture. It will put you on the road to true understanding and belief in yourself.

The Machinery of the Mind • We do a lot of things "automatically"—such as driving a car. But what happens when a person's mental machinery takes over and starts running him? In this fascinating lecture, L. Ron Hubbard gives you an understanding of what mental machinery really is, and how it can cause a person to lose control. You *can* regain your power of decision and be in full control of your life. Listen to this lecture and find out how.

The Affinity-Reality-Communication Triangle • Have you ever tried to talk to an angry man? Have you ever tried to get something across to someone who is really in fear? Have you ever known someone who was impossible to cheer up? Listen to this fascinating lecture by L. Ron Hubbard and learn how you can use the affinity-reality-communication triangle to resolve personal relationships. By using the data in this lecture, you can better understand others and live a happier life.

Increasing Efficiency • Inefficiency is a major barrier to success. How can you increase your efficiency? Is it a matter of changing your diet, or adjusting your working environment? These approaches have uniformly failed, because they overlook the most important element: *you*. L. Ron Hubbard has found those factors that *can* increase your efficiency, and he reveals it in this timely lecture. Get *Increasing Efficiency* now, and start achieving *your* full potential.

Man's Relentless Search • For countless centuries, man has been trying to find himself. Why does this quest repeatedly end in frustration and disappointment? What is he *really* looking for, and why can't he find it? For the real truth about man and life, listen to this taped lecture by L. Ron Hubbard, *Man's Relentless Search*. Restore your belief in yourself!

Advanced Scientology Cassettes

The Philadelphia Doctorate Course Lectures • This series of incomparable lectures, given by L. Ron Hubbard in Philadelphia in December 1952, tore the lid off the secrets of this universe. They reveal what you can do as a spiritual being who is superior to matter, energy, space and time.

The Route to Infinity Lectures • In these seven lectures, Ron bridges the gap between the ideal and the current scene—including data to help you create your future the way you want it.

The Phoenix Lectures • In this profound series of twenty-eight lectures, Ron presents the truth of man's nature as a spiritual being and his existence in the physical universe. Ron goes over the famous Axioms of Scientology in detail. He also covers time, the conditions of existence, the track of traditional wisdom on the planet and much more.

More advanced books and lectures are available. Contact your nearest organization or write directly to the publisher for a full catalog.

For more information about Scientology or to order books and cassettes

Call: 1-800-334-LIFE
in the US and Canada

Is there such a thing as a hot line that doesn't believe in giving advice? What about a hot line for able individuals to help them solve their *own* problems?

"If we take a man and keep giving him advice," L. Ron Hubbard has said, "we don't necessarily wind up with a resolution of his problems. But if, on the other hand, we put him in a position where he had higher intelligence, where his reaction time was better, where he could confront life better, where he could identify the factors in his life more easily, then he's in a position where he can solve his own problems."

Call the unique new hot line and referral service with operators trained in Scientology technology. Callers find someone they can trust to talk to about a problem, and they are referred to their nearest Scientology church or organization for more information if they are interested.

You can also order books and cassettes by L. Ron Hubbard by calling this number.

Call this toll-free number
7 days a week
from 9 A.M. to 11 P.M. Pacific Standard Time.

Get Your Free Catalog
of Knowledge on
How to Improve Life

L. Ron Hubbard's books and tapes increase your ability to understand yourself and others. His works give you the practical know-how you need to improve your life and the lives of your family and friends.

Many more materials by L. Ron Hubbard are available than have been covered in the pages of this book. A free catalog of these materials is available on request.

Write for your free catalog today!

Bridge Publications, Inc.
4751 Fountain Avenue
Los Angeles, California 90029

NEW ERA Publications International ApS
Store Kongensgade 55
1264 Copenhagen K, Denmark

"I am always happy to hear from my readers."
L. Ron Hubbard

These were the words of L. Ron Hubbard, who was always very interested in hearing from his friends and readers. He made a point of staying in communication with everyone he came in contact with over his fifty-year career as a professional writer, and he had thousands of fans and friends that he corresponded with all over the world.

The publishers of L. Ron Hubbard's works wish to continue this tradition and welcome letters and comments from you, his readers, both old and new.

Additionally, the publishers will be happy to send you information on anything you would like to know about Ron, his extraordinary life and accomplishments and the vast number of books he has written.

Any message addressed to the Author's Affairs Director at Bridge Publications will be given prompt and full attention.

Bridge Publications, Inc.
4751 Fountain Avenue
Los Angeles, California 90029
USA

Church and Organization Address List

United States of America

Albuquerque
Church of Scientology
8106 Menaul Blvd., NE
Albuquerque, New Mexico 87110

Ann Arbor
Church of Scientology
122 S. Main, Suite 160
Ann Arbor, Michigan 48106

Atlanta
Church of Scientology
2632 Piedmont Rd., NE
Atlanta, Georgia 30324

Austin
Church of Scientology
2200 Guadalupe
Austin, Texas 78705

Boston
Church of Scientology
448 Beacon Street
Boston, Massachusetts 02115

Buffalo
Church of Scientology
47 West Huron Street
Buffalo, New York 14202

Chicago
Church of Scientology
3011 North Lincoln Avenue
Chicago, Illinois 60657

Cincinnati
Church of Scientology
215 West 4th Street, 5th Floor
Cincinnati, Ohio 45202

Clearwater
Church of Scientology
Flag® Service Organization
210 South Fort Harrison Avenue
Clearwater, Florida 34616

Columbus
Church of Scientology
167 East State Street
Columbus, Ohio 43215

Dallas
Church of Scientology
Celebrity Centre® Dallas
8501 Manderville Lane
Dallas, Texas 75231

Denver
Church of Scientology
375 South Navajo Street
Denver, Colorado 80223

Detroit
Church of Scientology
321 Williams Street
Royal Oak, Michigan 48067

Honolulu
Church of Scientology
1 N. King St., Lower Level
Honolulu, Hawaii 96817

Kansas City
Church of Scientology
3619 Broadway
Kansas City, Missouri 64111

Las Vegas
Church of Scientology
846 East Sahara Avenue
Las Vegas, Nevada 89104

Church of Scientology
Celebrity Centre Las Vegas
1100 South 10th Street
Las Vegas, Nevada 89104

Long Island
Church of Scientology
330 Fulton Avenue
Hempstead, New York 11550

Los Angeles and vicinity
Church of Scientology
4810 Sunset Boulevard
Los Angeles, California 90027

Church of Scientology
1451 Irvine Boulevard
Tustin, California 92680

Church of Scientology
263 East Colorado Boulevard
Pasadena, California 91101

Church of Scientology
10335 Magnolia Boulevard
North Hollywood, California 91601

Church of Scientology
American Saint Hill Organization
1413 North Berendo Street
Los Angeles, California 90027

Church of Scientology
American Saint Hill Foundation
1413 North Berendo Street
Los Angeles, California 90027

Church of Scientology
Advanced Organization of
    Los Angeles
1306 North Berendo Street
Los Angeles, California 90027

Church of Scientology
Celebrity Centre International
5930 Franklin Avenue
Hollywood, California 90028

Miami
Church of Scientology
120 Giralda Avenue
Coral Gables, Florida 33134

Minneapolis
Church of Scientology
3019 Minnehaha Avenue
Minneapolis, Minnesota 55406

New Haven
Church of Scientology
909 Whalley Avenue
New Haven, Connecticut 06515

New York City
Church of Scientology
227 West 46th Street
New York City, New York 10036

Church of Scientology
Celebrity Centre New York
65 East 82nd Street
New York City, New York 10028

Orlando
Church of Scientology
710-A East Colonial Drive
Orlando, Florida 32803

Philadelphia
Church of Scientology
1315 Race Street
Philadelphia, Pennsylvania 19107

Phoenix
Church of Scientology
4450 North Central Avenue
Suite 102
Phoenix, Arizona 85012

Portland
Church of Scientology
323 SW Washington
Portland, Oregon 97204

Church of Scientology
Celebrity Centre Portland
709 Southwest Salmon Street
Portland, Oregon 97205

Sacramento
Church of Scientology
825 15th Street
Sacramento, California 95814

San Diego
Church of Scientology
701 "C" Street
San Diego, California 92101

San Francisco
Church of Scientology
83 McAllister Street
San Francisco, California 94102

San Jose
Church of Scientology
80 E. Rosemary
San Jose, California 95112

Santa Barbara
Church of Scientology
524 State Street
Santa Barbara, California 93101

Seattle
Church of Scientology
2603 3rd Street
Seattle, Washington 98121

St. Louis
Church of Scientology
9510 Page Boulevard
St. Louis, Missouri 63132

Tampa
Church of Scientology
4809 North Armenia Avenue
Suite 215
Tampa, Florida 33603

Washington, DC
Founding Church of Scientology
2125 "S" Street NW
Washington, DC 20008

Canada

Edmonton
Church of Scientology
10349 82nd Avenue
Edmonton, Alberta
Canada T6E 1Z9

Kitchener
Church of Scientology
8 Water Street North
Kitchener, Ontario
Canada N2H 5A5

Montréal
Church of Scientology
4489 Papineau Street
Montréal, Québec
Canada H2H 1T7

Ottawa
Church of Scientology
150 Rideau Street, 2nd Floor
Ottawa, Ontario
Canada K1N 5X6

Québec
Church of Scientology
350 Bd Chareste Est
Québec, Québec
Canada G1K 3H5

Toronto
Church of Scientology
696 Yonge Street, 2nd Floor
Toronto, Ontario
Canada M4Y 2A7

Vancouver
Church of Scientology
401 West Hastings Street
Vancouver, British Columbia
Canada V6B 1L5

Winnipeg
Church of Scientology
Suite 125–388 Donald Street
Winnipeg, Manitoba
Canada R3B 2J4

United Kingdom

Birmingham
Church of Scientology
60/62 Constitution Hill
Birmingham
England B19 3JT

Brighton
Church of Scientology
Dukes Arcade, Top Floor
Dukes Street
Brighton, Sussex
England BN1 1AG

East Grinstead
Saint Hill Foundation
Saint Hill Manor
East Grinstead, West Sussex
England RH19 4JY

Advanced Organization Saint Hill
Saint Hill Manor
East Grinstead, West Sussex
England RH19 4JY

Edinburgh
Hubbard Academy of Personal
    Independence
20 Southbridge
Edinburgh, Scotland EH1 1LL

London
Church of Scientology
68 Tottenham Court Road
London, England W1P 0BB

Manchester
Church of Scientology
258 Deansgate
Manchester, England M3 4BG

Plymouth
Church of Scientology
41 Ebrington Street
Plymouth, Devon
England PL4 9AA

Sunderland
Church of Scientology
51 Fawcett Street
Sunderland, Tyne and Wear
England SR1 1RS

Austria

Vienna
Church of Scientology
Schottenfeldgasse 13–15
1070 Vienna, Austria

Church of Scientology
Celebrity Centre Vienna
Senefeldergasse 11/5
1100 Vienna, Austria

Belgium

Brussels
Church of Scientology
45A, rue de l'Ecuyer
1000 Bruxelles, Belgium

Denmark

Aarhus
Church of Scientology
Guldsmedegade 17, 2
8000 Aarhus C, Denmark

Copenhagen
Church of Scientology
Store Kongensgade 55
1264 Copenhagen K, Denmark

Church of Scientology
Vesterbrogade 66
1620 Copenhagen V, Denmark

Church of Scientology
Advanced Organization Saint Hill
  for Europe and Africa
Jernbanegade 6
1608 Copenhagen V, Denmark

France

Angers
Church of Scientology
10–12, rue Max Richard
49000 Angers, France

Clermont-Ferrand
Church of Scientology
2 Pte rue Giscard de la Tour Fondue
63000 Clermont-Ferrand, France

Lyon
Church of Scientology
3, place des Capucins
69001 Lyon, France

Paris
Church of Scientology
65, rue de Dunkerque
75009 Paris, France

Church of Scientology
Celebrity Centre Paris
69, rue Legendre
75017 Paris, France

St. Etienne
Church of Scientology
24, rue Marengo
42000 St. Etienne, France

Germany

Berlin
Church of Scientology e.V.
Sponholzstrasse 51/52
1000 Berlin 41, Germany

Düsseldorf
Church of Scientology
Friedrichstrasse 28
4000 Düsseldorf, West Germany

Church of Scientology
Celebrity Centre Düsseldorf
Grupellostr. 28
4000 Düsseldorf, West Germany

Frankfurt
Church of Scientology
Darmstädter Landstrasse 213
6000 Frankfurt 70, West Germany

Hamburg
Church of Scientology e.V.
Steindamm 63
2000 Hamburg 1, West Germany

Church of Scientology
Celebrity Centre Hamburg
Mönckebergstrasse 5/IV
2000 Hamburg 1, West Germany

Hannover
Church of Scientology
Hubertusstrasse 2
D-3000 Hannover 1, West Germany

München
Church of Scientology e.V.
Beichstrasse 12
D-8000 München 40, West Germany

Stuttgart
Church of Scientology
Hirschstrasse 27
7000 Stuttgart 1, West Germany

Israel

Tel Aviv
Scientology and Dianetics College
7 Salomon Street
Tel Aviv 66023, Israel

Italy

Brescia
Church of Scientology
Dei Tre Laghi
Via Fratelli Bronzetti, 20
25125 Brescia, Italy

Catania
Church of Scientology
Via Giuseppe Garibaldi, 9
95121 Catania, Italy

Milano
Church of Scientology
Via Abetone, 10
20137 Milano, Italy

Monza
Church of Scientology
Via Cavour, 5
20052 Monza, Italy

Novara
Church of Scientology
Corso Cavallotti, 7
28100 Novara, Italy

Nuoro
Church of Scientology
Via G. Deledda, 43
08100 Nuoro, Italy

Padova
Church of Scientology
Via Mameli, 1/5
35131 Padova, Italy

Pordenone
Church of Scientology
Via Montereale, 10/C
33170 Pordenone, Italy

Roma
Church of Scientology
Via di San Vito, 11
00185 Roma, Italy

Torino
Church of Scientology
Via Guarini, 4
10121 Torino, Italy

Verona
Church of Scientology
Vicolo Chiodo, 4/A
37121 Verona, Italy

Netherlands

Amsterdam
Church of Scientology
Nieuwe Zijds Voorburgwal 271
1012 RL Amsterdam, Netherlands

Norway

Oslo
Church of Scientology
Storgata 9
0155 Oslo 1, Norway

Portugal

Lisbon
Instituto de Dianética
Rua Actor Taborda 39–4°
1000 Lisboa, Portugal

Spain

Barcelona
Dianética
Calle Pau Claris 85, Principal 1ª
08010 Barcelona, Spain

Madrid
Asociación Civil de Dianética
Montera 20, Piso 1° DCHA
28013 Madrid, Spain

Sweden

Göteborg
Church of Scientology
Odinsgatan 8
411 03 Göteborg, Sweden

Malmö
Church of Scientology
Simrishamnsgatan 10
21423 Malmö, Sweden

Stockholm
Church of Scientology
Kammakargatan 46
S-111 60 Stockholm, Sweden

Switzerland

Basel
Church of Scientology
Herrengrabenweg 56
4054 Basel, Switzerland

Bern
Church of Scientology
Schulhausgasse 12
3113 Rubigen
Bern, Switzerland

Genève
Church of Scientology
9 Route de Saint-Julien
1227 Carouge
Genève, Switzerland

Lausanne
Church of Scientology
10, rue de la Madeleine
1003 Lausanne, Switzerland

Zürich
Church of Scientology
Badenerstrasse 294
CH-8004 Zürich, Switzerland

Australia

Adelaide
Church of Scientology
24 Waymouth Street
Adelaide, South Australia 5000
Australia

Brisbane
Church of Scientology
2nd Floor, 106 Edward Street
Brisbane, Queensland 4000
Australia

Canberra
Church of Scientology
Suite 16, 108 Bunda Street
Civic Canberra
A.C.T. 2601, Australia

Melbourne
Church of Scientology
44 Russell Street
Melbourne, Victoria 3000
Australia

Perth
Church of Scientology
39–41 King Street
Perth, Western Australia 6000
Australia

Sydney
Church of Scientology
201 Castlereagh Street
Sydney, New South Wales 2000
Australia

Church of Scientology
Advanced Organization Saint Hill
    Australia, New Zealand and
    Oceania
19–37 Greek Street
Glebe, New South Wales 2037
Australia

Japan

Tokyo

Scientology Organization
101 Toyomi Nishi Gotanda Heights
2-13-5 Nishi Gotanda
Shinagawa-ku
Tokyo, Japan 141

New Zealand

Auckland

Church of Scientology
32 Lorne Street
Auckland 1, New Zealand

Africa

Bulawayo

Church of Scientology
74 Abercorn Street
Bulawayo, Zimbabwe

Cape Town

Church of Scientology
5 Beckham Street
Gardens
Cape Town 8001, South Africa

Durban

Church of Scientology
57 College Lane
Durban 4001, South Africa

Harare

Church of Scientology
First Floor State Lottery Building
PO Box 3524
Corner Speke Avenue and
    Julius Nyerere Way
Harare, Zimbabwe

Johannesburg

Church of Scientology
Security Building, 2nd Floor
95 Commissioner Street
Johannesburg 2001, South Africa

Church of Scientology
101 Huntford Building
40 Hunter Street
Cnr. Hunter and Fortesque Roads
Yeoville 2198
Johannesburg, South Africa

Port Elizabeth

Church of Scientology
2 St. Christopher
27 Westbourne Road
Central
Port Elizabeth 6001, South Africa

Pretoria

Church of Scientology
1st Floor City Centre
272 Pretorius Street
Pretoria 0002, South Africa

Latin America

Colombia

Bogotá

Centro Cultural de Dianética
Carrera 19 No. 39–55
Apartado Aereo 92419
Bogotá, D.E. Colombia

Mexico

Guadalajara

Organización Cultural Dianética de
    Guadalajara, A.C.
Av. Lopez Mateos Nte. 329
Sector Hidalgo
Guadalajara, Jalisco,
México

Mexico City

Asociación Cultural Dianética, A.C.
Hermes No. 46
Colonia Crédito Constructor
03940 México, D.F.

Instituto de Filosofia Aplicada, A.C.
Durango #105
Colonia Roma
06700 México, D.F.

Instituto de Filosofia Aplicada, A.C.
Plaza Rio de Janeiro No. 52
Colonia Roma
06700 México, D.F.

Instituto Technologico de
    Dianética, A.C.
Londres 38-5to piso
Colonia Juarez
C.P. 06600 México, D.F.

Organización, Desarrollo y
    Dianética, A.C.
Providencia 1000
Colonia Del Valle
C.P. 03100 México, D.F.

Centro de Dianética Polanco
Insurgentes Sur 536, 1er piso
    Esq. Nogales
Colonia Roma Sur
C.P. 06700 México, D.F.

Venezuela

Valencia

Asociación Cultural Dianética de
    Venezuela, A.C.
Avenida 101 No. 150–23
Urbanizacion La Alegria
Apartado Postal 833
Valencia, Venezuela

To obtain any books or cassettes by L. Ron Hubbard which are not available at your local organization, contact any of the following publishers:

Bridge Publications, Inc.
4751 Fountain Avenue
Los Angeles, California 90029

Continental Publications Liaison
    Office
696 Yonge Street
Toronto, Ontario
Canada M4Y 2A7

NEW ERA Publications
    International ApS
Store Kongensgade 55
1264 Copenhagen K, Denmark

Era Dinámica Editores, S.A. de C.V.
Alabama 105
Colonia Nápoles
C.P. 03810 México, D.F.

NEW ERA Publications, Ltd.
78 Holmethorpe Avenue
Redhill, Surrey RH1 2NL
England

N.E. Publications Australia Pty. Ltd.
2 Verona Street
Paddington, New South Wales 2021
Australia

Continental Publications Pty. Ltd.
PO Box 27080
Benrose
2011 South Africa

NEW ERA Publications Italia Srl
Via L.G. Columella, 12
20128 Milano, Italy

NEW ERA Publications GmbH
Otto—Hahn—Strasse 25
6072 Dreieich 1, Germany

NEW ERA Publications France
111, boulevard de Magenta
75010 Paris, France

New Era Publications España, S.A.
C/De la Paz, 4/1° DCHA
28012 Madrid, Spain

New Era Publications Japan, Inc.
5-4-5-803 Nishi Gotanda
Shinagawa-ku
Tokyo, Japan 141

521